THE SOUL - AN INQUIRY

Francis Selman

The Soul - An Inquiry

ST PAULS

ST PAULS Publishing
187 Battersea Bridge Road, London SW11 3AS, UK

Copyright © Francis Selman

ISBN 085439 686 1

Set by LcL Graphics, London
Printed by Interprint Ltd, Marsa, Malta

ST PAULS is an activity of the priests and brothers of the Society
of St Paul who proclaim the Gospel through the media of social
communication

CONTENTS

To Ruth Agnes

INTRODUCTION

'What is man that you think of him, the son of man that you care for him?' the Psalmist asks.[1] One of the effects of natural science, which is the study of nature, in our day has been to lead us away from nature, so that many people no longer have much awareness of it in their daily life. As our knowledge of so many features of the world becomes ever more exact, we are in danger of forgetting our own nature. What is a human being? What am I? Am I just a material body, whose thoughts are merely the result of physical reactions in the brain, as many philosophers and scientists hold today? Or is what I really am quite separate from my body, a soul or a self, as dualists suppose? Or is a human being in some way a unity of body and soul, as I hope to show? Do I only exist for as long as my life lasts in this world and then come to an end altogether, or do I survive in some form after death? And when we inquire about the origin of human beings, has their power of reasoning and thinking merely arisen as the highest stage of an evolutionary process from matter alone, which does not require any further explanation beyond the material universe we inhabit? These are just some of the questions we can ask about the nature of human beings.

Pope John Paul II observes that we find in the ancient writers of East and West alike three great questions: Who am I? Where do I come from? And where am I going to?[2] They are none other than the questions of my identity, my origin and my destiny. They are the great questions of our own time, as they have been of every age. In a seemingly prophetic way, one of the great scientists of the 20th century, Erwin Schrödinger, who had no religious belief, asked the very same questions almost

50 years earlier, in 1950. In Schrödinger's view, the aim and value of natural science is as it helps us to answer the age-old question: 'And who are we?' 'I am born into an environment - I know not whence I came nor whither I go nor who I am'.[3] But he did not believe that the answer to these questions could depend on the measurements of quantity that are the scientist's way of describing the world. It is, as he says, a philosophical question.

The key to answering these questions is the *soul*. Without a soul, human beings are in the last resort purely material, for without the soul no other explanation of the mind is left than the body. Unless I have a soul that has been created by God, I have come about purely by physical generation. And, unless I have an immaterial soul, I clearly do not continue to exist after my body dies. Although the soul was part of the common view of human beings from ancient until quite recent times, we have almost ceased to speak about the soul today. There are two main reasons for this. First, the prevailing outlook of our time is materialist: many find it hard to believe that anything really exists except what we have the evidence of the senses for and natural science studies. Secondly, belief in an immaterial soul seems inevitably to go with dualism, which many philosophers today are determined to banish. In this book, I want to show how it is possible to hold that we have an immortal soul without being a dualist. This view will match the biblical view of human beings.

The first thing revealed to us in Scripture about human beings is that they are made *in the image of God*: 'Let us make man in our image, after our likeness'.[4] We obviously are not made in the image of God in our bodies, for God is not material but pure spirit. So the image of God in us must lie in some immaterial aspect of our nature, in which the body may also share. According to Christian tradition, this image lies in the soul or mind. This was the thought of St Augustine:

> No one can doubt that man has been made in the image
> of Him who created him, not according to the body,
> nor according to any part of the mind, but according

to the rational mind where the knowledge of God can reside.[5]

We notice that Scripture says, 'Let us make man in *our* image', as though God were more than one person. We are not just made in the image of God, then, but of the Trinity. We know and love ourselves, just as God knows and loves himself. In his understanding of himself, God begets a perfect concept of his own nature, the Word, who is his Son. The Holy Spirit is the Love of God, who proceeds from the Father and the Son in the mutual love of one another. It is because we are made in the image of God that we have the capacity to know and love him; no other kind of visible creature is able to know and love its Creator. St Augustine thought that we are in the image of God in the mind, because it is with the mind that we can know God.

Another reason why we are in the image of God is that what makes us in his image, the rational soul, comes directly from him by a special creation. In the second account of the creation of man, we are told that when God had fashioned Adam's body from the earth he breathed the breath of life into him 'and man became a living being'.[6] This has traditionally been taken to mean that the human soul comes from God. What makes us spiritual beings, as distinct from merely bodily or material beings, comes directly from God.

St Paul clearly had this verse of *Genesis* in mind when he summed up the biblical view of human beings in his famous chapter on the resurrection:

> An ensouled body is sown, a spiritual body is raised up.
> Thus it is written: the first Adam became a living soul,
> the last Adam a life-giving spirit. The spiritual is not
> first but the ensouled, then comes the spiritual.[7]

Where the standard translations have 'natural' I have put 'ensouled', because the word used by St Paul is not *physikon*, which would mean 'natural', but *psuchikon*, the adjective from *psuche*, which means soul. The biblical view of human beings, in the Old as in the New Testament, is that we are ensouled bodies. The real 'me' is not just my soul, for the body also is an essential part of what I am by nature. Thus the Bible presents us with a *unified* view of human beings. This same unified view was put forward at the Second Vatican Council, when the Church did not hesitate to speak of the soul in saying,

> Man, though made of body and soul, is a unity.[8]

Thus the soul remains a part of the Church's understanding of what a human being is. St Peter tells us that we should be ready to give a reason (*logos*) for the hope that is in us.[9] My aim in the following chapters is to present the reasons why we should continue to speak of the soul, so that we shall be able to give to our contemporaries an account of our hope in the next life.

The soul is often passed over today, because many assume that it is a religious term which is, therefore, of little interest to those who have no religion. Aristotle, however, shows us that it is possible to discuss the soul in a purely philosophical way without presupposing any religious belief. Indeed, he shows us how we may come to the idea of the soul just by asking about the origin of life, quite apart from any requirements for belief in an after-life. The soul can be discussed in a purely philosophical way, because it is a part of our *nature*. We can know about nature by the natural light of reason. Thus the greater part of this book is a philosophical inquiry into the soul. Only in the last chapter, when I come to discuss the next life, do I make use of Scripture in showing that reason leads us to what the Christian faith believes about immortality and the resurrection.

It would be strange if we inquired about the nature of all the other things in the universe, which we study in natural science, but we did not inquire about our own nature. Thus Aristotle not only says that it is a noble thing to inquire about the soul, for it concerns the nature of the very beings who study and ask about the rest of the universe, but this inquiry about the soul will also make a contribution to natural science itself.

> Supposing that knowledge is a noble and valuable thing, then an inquiry into the soul is a noble pursuit because knowledge of the soul is thought to make a great contribution to understanding the truth and especially to the knowledge of nature.[10]

The Greek word for knowledge, *episteme*, also means science. Thus an inquiry into the soul can contribute to science because, as we noted above in the words of Schrödinger, the end of natural science is to come to a greater understanding of ourselves, what or who we are.

In chapters One and Two I first give an outline of the two main alternative views of human beings: dualism and materialism. In chapter Three, I introduce Aristotle's theory of the soul as the form of the body, which has been the best way of explaining the unity of body and soul. In chapter Four, I argue that, as natural science has not been able to explain the rise of life or consciousness, it has not rendered the concept of the soul unnecessary. In the Fifth chapter I argue that, as the mind is not material, it must be the power of something else than the body - of the soul. In the Sixth chapter, I discuss the unity of the body and soul. In asking after the origin of the soul, I argue in the Seventh chapter that, as it cannot be explained as the product of language or culture, it comes 'from outside'. Since the origin of everyone's soul may well account for the uniqueness of every human being, the Ninth chapter is taken up with a discussion of what is a person. This provides the foundation for seeing, in the final chapter, what is required for the same person to survive after this life. This involves questions about the resurrection of the body as well as the immortality of the soul.

NOTES

[1]   *Ps* 8,4.

[2]   *Faith and Reason* 1.

[3]   *Nature and the Greeks and Science and Humanism* (Cambridge 1996) 108.

[4]   *Gen* 1, 26.

[5]   *De Trinitate IX* 7, 12

[6]   *Gen* 2, 7.

[7]   *1 Cor* 15, 44-46.

[8]   *Gaudium et spes* 14.

[9]   *1 Pet* 3,15.

[10] *De Anima I* c.1 402a 1.

1

DUALISM

There are three main questions about the soul. Do we have a soul? Is the soul immortal? And how is it related to the body? If the soul is material there is little difficulty about the unity of the body and soul, and no question of its immortality, since being material it perishes with the body. But if the soul is immortal it is immaterial and can exist on its own after death as something substantial in itself. Here there is a difficulty about the relation of the soul to the body. Those who have held that the soul is immaterial have thus divided into two groups: some, like Plato, have taught that we consist of two quite separate things, a body and a soul. This is the dualist view. Others, like Aristotle, have seen a unity of body and soul, because the soul is related to the body as its form.

Nearly everyone in the ancient world thought that we have a soul. Many of them, however, perhaps the majority, then as now, thought that it was material. They supposed that, since the soul is invisible and present throughout the body, it consisted of tiny particles of one of the four elements that the ancients thought everything was made of, except earth. Thus Thales (c. 625-545 B.C.) said it consisted of water, Anaximenes (c. 550 -500 B.C.) of air, and Heraclitus (c. 500) of fire. We recognize why anyone should have thought that the soul consists of water, because all living things need water; and of air, because all animate things breathe and when a human being breathes his or her last breath, the spirit or soul seems to go out of them. It was thought to be like fire, because some of the ancients held that the soul was a spark of the divine nature or mind in us.

This sort of materialist view of the soul persisted down to the 17th century, for we find Descartes telling us that at first it was his view:

> But as to the nature of the soul, either it did not attract my attention, or else I fancied something subtle like air or fire or aether mingled among the grosser parts of the body.[1]

Augustine, however, had this to say about ancient materialist views of the soul:

> If the soul is air, when the soul understands, air understands. We know that we understand but we do not think that fire thinks.[2]

Augustine himself thought that the soul is quite immaterial. One reason he gives is that the mind differs in nature from its images, since it is able to distinguish between external bodies and the images it has of them.[3] If the mind was just like its images, it could not make judgements about them.

Plato

The first writer to set out the view that the soul is immaterial was Plato (427-347 B.C.). We find this view in his early dialogue, the *Phaedo*, which presents the discussion that Socrates is supposed to have held with some of his friends a few hours before his death. So he asks them what they think happens at death. They reply that some think the soul vanishes into thin air but the followers of Pythagoras hold that death is the release of the soul from its imprisonment in the body. Socrates then assures his friends that he has no need to fear death, because he can show them that the soul does not die but continues to live.

He does this by first arguing that all learning in this life is really the reminiscence of ideas one knew in a previous existence before coming into this world. His proof for this is the example of a slave boy who gives the right answers when he is questioned by Socrates and thus shows that he possesses

the ideas of geometry, although he has never been taught any
geometry. By putting questions in a certain order, Socrates gets
the slave to see that the way to construct a square twice the
area of the original square is not to lengthen the sides of the
original square but to construct a square on the diagonal of the
original square, so that the triangular half of the first square
becomes a quarter of the new square. This is Socrates', or Plato's
argument for innate ideas: that is, we are born with ideas rather
than acquire them for the first time in this life. The soul already
possesses ideas because it pre-exists. And if the soul pre-exists
this life, it can also exist on its own after it has left the body.
Thus Socrates' argument for the immortality of the soul rests
on its pre-existence. He also draws a comparison of the soul
with the senses: as the senses are material like the things which
they perceive, so the soul is immaterial like the ideas which it
knows.[4] Since immaterial things cannot be cut up into parts or
divided like material bodies, for they have no parts, the soul that
is immaterial is also simple and indestructible. Thus Plato is the
first to state the argument that the soul is immortal because it is
simple (without parts).

Socrates, however, admits that his argument for the
immortality of the soul stands or falls with the existence of the
Ideas, which the soul is supposed to know before it enters the
body. For obviously one cannot argue that the soul pre-exists
since it already knows ideas before this life, if the Ideas do not
exist. Few people today probably hold Plato's theory of the
Ideas that exist on their own as real objects in an invisible and
immaterial world. Indeed, Plato himself began to criticize his
own theory later in his life because he says that, if the Ideas
could exist on their own, they would have to be active in some
way. They could not just be thought but would also have to be
thinking, and so be minds, if they were to have an existence on
their own, independently of people thinking of them.

Socrates thought that the alternative to his view of the soul
was the Harmony Theory, which says that the soul is a harmony
composed of the elements of the body. As the harmony of a
lyre consists in the condition of its strings, so the soul is the
composition of the elements of the body, which it holds together.

This theory of the soul does not allow for its immortality because, if the soul is the harmony of the body, it can no more continue to exist when the body disintegrates than a tune can the moment the strings of the lyre are broken. Also, if the soul were the harmony of the body, it would not cause movement but be produced by the movement of the body, just as a harmony is produced by the movement of the strings. The soul, however, is commonly thought to be the source of the body's movement, because inanimate matter cannot move unless it is moved by something else, but a living body is the source of its own motion. The Harmony Theory of the soul was widely held in the ancient world, among others by the great physician Galen (2nd century A.D.). A form of this theory has recently been put forward by John Polkinghorne, who describes the soul as 'the complex information-bearing pattern carried by the ever changing array of atoms that make up our bodies'.[5]

Plato rejected the Harmony Theory, because a harmony does not move the strings but is produced by their movement; so the soul that is a harmony does not control the body but follows it. This, however, is contrary to experience, for when we resist our passions and control our emotions the soul does not follow but *rules* the body.[6] Aristotle, too, rejected the Harmony Theory, because he did not think we could say what the composition of the elements of the intellect, or understanding, would be like. This criticism of the Harmony Theory also applies to materialist theories of the mind today. We may also remark that, if the soul is a harmony of the body, it cannot transcend the qualities of its material elements.

In another dialogue, however, Plato gives a good argument why the soul *transcends* the body. He first compares a human being with the Trojan horse. Just as there were men inside the Trojan horse who looked at the world outside through holes in its underside, so we perceive the world through the senses of the body. But we are not just like the Trojan horse, because each of the men inside the horse had his own *separate* perception of the world, but we are able to combine the various sensations we have at the same time and so have *one* experience through the perceptions of the different senses. As this cannot be explained by any one of the senses, for each sense only perceives its own objects and does not know what belongs to the other senses (the ear cannot perceive colour or the eyes sound or taste), it must be by something different from the sense. We might say that this is done by the brain, which receives messages from all the senses and so combines them. But Socrates then asks how it is possible to reflect on sensation itself, which is to think about what is common to all the senses. This cannot be by a sense. Socrates argues that, as the senses have bodily organs, but it is not by the senses we can know what sensation is itself, so we do not know this by anything corporeal.

He then proposes to Theaetetus, in this same dialogue: 'Let us take a colour and a sound'. We know that each exists, that each by itself is one and together they are two or many; that each is the same as itself and different from the other. These propositions give us the five ideas of existence, unity, multitude, similarity and difference. We call these 'transcendental' ideas, because they run through anything that we speak about. Again, whatever can know things in a way that transcends the senses cannot be material like them. Finally, Socrates asks how we know what can be said of anything we talk about, that it is or is not, that it is true or false. We do not apprehend truth by the senses but by reasoning. Animals, for example, just have images but they do not know or ask whether they are true or false. Theaetetus replies that we do not know truth or falsehood by means of any special organ, but 'the soul considers these things by itself'.[7] Although modern translations have 'mind' instead of 'soul' here, we should not translate psuche with what we take to be our equivalent for soul today when Greek has another word for mind (nous). In these two connected passages of the Theaetetus, then, Plato provides us with an argument for the existence of the soul and that the soul is not material like the senses, otherwise we could not reflect on sensation or have the transcendental ideas. This argument still stands even when we do not accept Plato's argument for the immortality of the soul in the Phaedo.

Plato's dualist view of human beings remained the dominant one among Christian writers for over one thousand years.

His theory of the soul was attractive to Christians, because it provided a clear argument for immortality. This was not so clear with Aristotle's theory of the soul, because it is not so easy to show that the soul survives when it is the form of the body. In the thirteenth century, however, St Albert the Great (c. 1200-1280), followed by his pupil St Thomas Aquinas, took up Aristotle's theory of the soul as the form of the body because it provided a unified view of human beings that was more in keeping with the biblical view. Aristotle's theory also had the advantage of making more sense of the resurrection of the body, since it makes the body an essential part of a human being. Thus Aristotle's view was also better adapted to a religion which uses sacraments with material signs. Aristotle's theory of the unity of body and soul then superseded the Platonist view until the sixteenth century, when the scientific discoveries of Kepler, Galileo and others showed that the physics of Aristotle was wrong. When Aristotle's natural science was rejected, much of the rest of his philosophy went out too. The way was then left open for the return of Plato's dualism with Descartes (c. 1596-1650). It was all the easier for Descartes to separate the soul from the body and confine it to the mental, because the newly discovered laws of mechanics seemed to explain the movement of the body apart from the soul.

Descartes

Unlike Plato, Descartes was not first concerned with the immortality of the soul but with the question of what *he* was. This in turn was part of his search for a starting-point of knowledge that could not be doubted, in other words, for something he could be certain about. In order to establish an unshakeable foundation of knowledge, he assumes nothing and doubts the existence of everything familiar around him, including his own body. He found, however, that even when he supposed his body to be an illusion, in other words that *he* did not really have a body, he was still aware that he existed. This at least was something he could be certain of. He reasoned that whatever is aware that it exists must be something, but, as this could not be a body, since he supposed that he was unaware of his body, he came to the conclusion that he must be something without a body, which he called a *res cogitans*, a thinking thing or substance. Descartes divided all substances in the world into thinking, or conscious, ones and extended ones (*res extensa*). A body was an extended substance for Descartes, as all bodies have dimensions that can be measured. For Descartes, to be conscious meant to be aware that one exists, which only beings with self - reflection are. Consciousness for Descartes is the awareness of *oneself* rather than of other things around one. Consequently, Descartes denied that animals are conscious, because they do not have self-reflection. This led him to think that they do not have pain, which contradicts our observation of them.

There seems to be little doubt that Descartes thought that what he really was something incorporeal and immaterial, that is, his soul. 'What is this 'I' of whose existence I am aware?' he asks, and replies: "I am' precisely taken refers only to a conscious being; that is a mind, a soul, an intellect'.[8] In a letter he altogether denies that he is a corporeal being with a body: 'this conscious I is an immaterial substance with no corporeal element'.[9] Thus Descartes separates the soul from the body and isolates us in a mental world divorced from the natural world, of which our bodies are a part.

By making consciousness, the awareness of oneself, rather than life the primary characteristic of the soul, he dissolved the connection of the soul with the body, which he then came to regard as a mere machine. For Descartes, the body by itself resembles a machine that can carry on all its operations that do not depend on the command of the will 'even if there is no mind in it'.[10] Thus Descartes' view of a human being has been described as that of 'the Ghost in a Machine'. It is a paradox that Descartes' view of himself as a soul has resulted in our being regarded as just machines today.

Nonetheless, however much our body may resemble machines in the complexity of its structure, it has more in common with living creatures than it does with any machine, because it has *life*. Interestingly, there is no tendency to say that the bodies of simple living things are like machines.

Descartes divides the source of our vital activities and, hence, the unity of a human being when he says the body is like a machine that can carry out operations 'even if there is no mind in it', and keeps the soul for thoughts alone. Thoughts (*cogitationes*), however, include sensations for Descartes, but not dreams, because we are not conscious when we have these. It is plain that there must be a union of body and soul, because volitions, which are mental events, directly cause movements of the body. For example, when a musician draws her bow over the strings of her violin, this movement of her arms and hands is caused by her *will*. For Aristotle, however, there is a *single* principle of all our vital activities, which include thinking and digesting: 'the soul is that by which we primarily live and perceive and think'.[11] There is not a separate source of thinking from moving and seeing in me.

What should we say about Descartes' dualism? First, it is not so easy to be unaware of one's body as Descartes supposed, when it is the body that you are thinking you are not aware of. Descartes argument for being certain about at least one thing, that he exists, leads to solipsism, because if I suppose that all the bodies of people I see walking around me are illusions, there is no reason to think that there is anyone with a mind around me. It would only be possible to think there were other minds if we could know them directly, which we cannot in this world. Solipsism is the view that, because I only know what is in my own mind, I am the only mind.

Elizabeth Anscombe points out that, since Descartes doubted the existence of his body, he ought to have doubted the existence of the *man* which other people called René Descartes, because a man (or human being) is something with a body.[12] This clearly is dualism, to think that what you really are, your soul, is quite different from the body by which other people know you. It gives rise to thinking that what I am is something other than what the rest of people call René Descartes, or whatever your name is. Descartes forgot that he could not have had the thought 'I think, therefore I am' (*cogito, ergo sum*) unless he had first learnt the words with which he had this thought. But I only learn words by hearing with the ears of my body the sounds that other people utter with their mouths. We only learn language and communicate our thoughts to others with the body. Thus the body is an integral part of the way human beings think, and it is not possible to isolate our minds in a purely mental world. It was inconsistent of Descartes to say that a thinking thing, like the soul, has thoughts and to include sensations among them because I am conscious of them, when having sensations involves the body. Although sensation belongs to the soul inasmuch as a body without a soul has no sensation, there is no sensation without a body because it requires the bodily organs of the senses.

Although dualism has taken a severe knocking in the past four decades, it is not without its adherents today and may even be making a slight comeback in English circles. For example, the philosopher of science, Karl Popper, recognized that there is a clear distinction between the mind and body, because my thoughts are quite different from anything that is going on in me physically. One cannot locate thoughts in the body or trace them with X-rays. Popper divides the world into three strata, which he called World One, Two and Three. World One is the world of inanimate objects, World Two the world of conscious beings, including animals, and World Three the world of thought, art, culture and scientific theories. This third world is just as real, Popper says, as World One, because it influences human beings and has an affect on the physical world. My self is largely the product of World Three, in Popper's view. When we talk about the contents of a book we do not mean its pages but the *thoughts* it contains. The thoughts and ideas of sculptors and architects make a difference to the visible face of the material world. Popper, however, did not think that the soul is anything substantial. This leaves us asking how the mind can be so distinct from the body as Popper thought it was when there is nothing for it to be the power of. If the cause of thought is not material, as Popper held it was not, it must be due to something else than the body. The alternative is to give a materialist explanation of the mind, as do the majority of philosophers and scientists today. Thus we now turn to some versions of materialism in the next chapter.

NOTES

1   *Meditation II.*

2   *De Trinitate X* 10,13.

3   *Ibid. X* 5,7.

4   *Phaedo* 79b.

5   *Science and Creation* (London 1988) 72.

6   *Phaedo* 94 C.

7   *Theaetetus* 185d (*aute di'hautes he psuche*).

8   *Meditation II, Descartes Philosophical Writings* trans. G.E.M. Anscombe and P.T. Geach 69.

9   Correspondence 219, trans. Anscombe and Geach 263.

10 *Meditation VI,* 120.

11 *De Anima II* c.2 414a 10

12 *Collected Philosophical Papers* vol. II 22.

2

MATERIALISM

As we have already noted, the materialist view of human beings was widespread in ancient times. The difference between ancient and modern materialism is that materialists of the ancient world thought that the soul consisted of tiny particles of matter, like air, water or fire; but modern materialists leave out the soul altogether and say all our activities, including thinking, can be explained physically. In this chapter, I propose to look at four versions of the materialist view of the mind: the Identity Theory theory, that the mind can be explained by the brain, that the mind is like a computer, and that thought is a property of the brain.

1. The Identity Theory

Materialist theories of the mind today hold that mental events are either caused by, or are nothing other than, physical processes of the brain. Mental events include thoughts and sensations, as though these two were the same kind of phenomenon, whereas they need to be distinguished. The ancient Greeks, for example, thought that sensation and the mind (*nous*) were quite distinct; they would never have called sensation 'mental', as many do today. The most thorough-going of these theories is the Identity Theory, which holds that mental events are identical with events in the brain. According to this view, thought can be explained like sensation as purely physical processes in the brain and nervous system. No other events occur in us except changes in material states of the body and brain. The case for this theory rests on the likelihood of showing the correlation between thoughts and events in the brain. There are, however, major difficulties in the way of showing this. First, we would have to show that the same brain event *always* goes with the same thought if the theory is to be strictly true. We can only identify mental states with physical ones if we know what we are looking for, but which states are embodied in physical ones is not something that science tells us but our ordinary self-understanding. Thus our understanding of ourselves *precedes* any attempt to explain it by science.

Secondly, as only I know which thought is in my mind at any moment, the only way it would be possible to establish that a certain event in the brain was identical with a particular thought would be for me to observe, by means of instruments, what was going on in my brain. But even if it were possible for me to correlate events in my brain with my passing thoughts, another difficulty would arise, for at the same time as I had a thought, say 'London is on the river Thames', I would also have a second thought, that this event in the brain I am now observing is identical with my thought 'London is on the river Thames'. In order to show that the Identity Theory is true, I would then have to correlate the second thought, that this event recorded by the instruments is identical with the original thought 'London is on the river Thames' with a reaction in the brain, but this could never be done; I would have to observe two events in the brain simultaneously with having the corresponding thoughts.

To think that the movement I observe in the dials that record what happens in my brain, manifests my thoughts is to reflect on one's perceptions and thoughts. We cannot, however, reflect on ourselves if the mind is material, because no part of a material body can bend back on itself but only on other parts. The fifth century philosopher, Proclus, remarked that nothing material can reflect on itself, since to reflect on itself is to revert to itself; but no material body can revert upon itself with the whole of itself, as the mind can.[1] A material part cannot turn back on itself, as the mind does in reflecting on its activities of thinking, seeing, desiring, fearing, deciding, reckoning and so on. Proclus' argument has been recently revived by Lloyd

Gerson, who points out that knowing that I am seeing is a different state from the state of seeing itself. He argues that, if mental states were identical with states of the brain, we could never know that we were in those states; we would just have the states without being able to reflect on them.

One could object that self-reflection need not be immaterial, because a machine could be said to reflect on itself when it simultaneously monitors and checks its own operations. This seems to be an example of something material reflecting on itself. But this differs from what we mean by self-reflection, because a machine does this with one part of itself on another, but I reflect on myself as a whole. The part of the machine cannot monitor itself, but when I reflect on myself I also know that I am reflecting on myself. Also, a machine does not know that it exists or that it is a machine, but to be conscious of oneself is to know that one exists. If animals do not have self-reflection, much less do machines, which do not even have imagination.

These arguments also apply to those who say that self-reflection is a self-scanning mechanism of the central nervous system.[2] If mental events were the same as physical events, when the brain scanned itself it would scan physical states. But we are not aware of the states of our nervous system or brain when we have thoughts and sensations. It is only possible to scan physical states of the brain by external means, but self-reflection is an intrinsic activity of the mind, not done by means of something else. The same difficulty of explaining self-reflection is met by our next version of a materialist theory of mind. This is the expectation that when we understand the way the brain works by neurophysiology, we shall also be able to explain the mind.

2. Neuroscience

A common version of the materialist theory today is what may be called a scientific explanation of the mind. A typical proponent of this approach is Sir Francis Crick, who discovered the double helix structure of DNA with James Watson in 1953. Crick holds that there is nothing more to our thoughts, decisions and sensations than what goes on in the neurons of our brain. He believes that by studying one aspect of consciousness we will be able to explain all aspects of it. For his special study he has selected sight, because we are above all visual creatures and often use words connected with seeing for the mind's understanding. Crick's question is: How do we see things the way that we see them? How do things appear three-dimensional when the image on the retina is flat? He admits, however, that it still is not possible to explain how the brain forms a unified picture in vision.[3] The psychiatrist Oliver Sacks confirms that we do not know exactly how a unified image is formed but says that some integrating must occur, which is 'totally inexplicable by any existing theory'.[4] If we cannot yet explain seeing completely, we are still a long way from explaining the mind by what goes on in the brain.

There is more to explaining the mind than seeing. For example, when I look at a watch I can see it in several ways: I can see it as bits of metal and perspex with a leather strap, or as *one* thing, or as an instrument for telling the time, which is to have the idea of its *purpose*. But it is hard to explain how we come to have the idea of purpose if our minds have come from matter, because matter does not move of itself for a purpose. Matter does not know what it is doing or why it is doing what it does. One may deny that there is any purpose or teleology displayed in nature, although this rather goes against the evidence, but not that we have the idea of purpose and do many things for a purpose.

If it were true that all our thoughts can be explained by electrical impulses passing through the cells of our brain across the synapses that connect them, there should be a special set of neurons for knowing the truth as there is a special area at the back of the brain for seeing, since knowing that what one knows is true differs from just seeing things as they are. It is to know that one's mind agrees with the real world. But no one suggests that there is a special part of the brain for knowing that our perceptions are true. It seems that, on the contrary, as all activity in the brain is caused by stimuli received from the senses, our thoughts would never rise above the sensory information received by the brain if the mind were just the brain.

How could *internal* reflection on our sensations and thoughts arise if thoughts were solely cause by stimuli *to* the brain?

Crick admits that the greatest obstacle to a scientific explanation of the mind is what are called *qualia* (from *qualis*, which sort or kind?). The difference between the sound of a violin and cello is not just a matter of the frequency of their sound waves, which can be registered on a dial. We can tell what they are like, although an instrument cannot register the difference of tone. We describe sounds as harsh and mellow, colours as warm and rich. Science measures the quantitative, not the qualitative. It is unable to explain why music delights.

3. Like Computers

A third way of explaining the mind materially is to say that it is like a computer. This version of materialism supposes that, because computers can perform some of the operations of intelligent beings, therefore the mind is material like the computers. There are many points to be remarked about this view. First, we are not like computers but they are like their makers, just as a duke is not said to be like his portrait but his portrait like him. Secondly, this view trades on the fallacy of saying that, since computers can perform the operations of intelligent beings, therefore our intelligence could have arisen from matter. Elizabeth Anscombe remarked about this view that our ability to make computers is meant to show that there is no need to suppose that human intelligence comes from an Intelligent Being. As we can make computers to perform intellectual operations like calculating by arranging pieces of matter, so intelligent beings could have arisen by the chance arrangement of matter in the course of evolution. This argument, however, overlooks a crucial point: we have made computers to carry out *logical* operations, but logical actions are not explained by matter arranging itself. Anscombe draws the conclusion that, as computers presuppose the intelligence of their makers, so perhaps the intelligent nature of their makers comes from an Intelligence too.[5]

Even though computers do 'intelligent' operations, they have no understanding. A computer divides but it does not know what division is, because it does not have the concept of division. A computer may be able to play chess better than most human beings, but no computer has thought of making a computer that can play chess or ever invented a game like chess.

Just because we possess the formal systems of mathematics and logic does not mean that we are like things that operate with a formal system, for we are the source of the formal systems in the machines we construct to work with them. It does not follow that our minds are material like things that work with formal systems; we still have to explain how we could think of these formal systems in the first place.

In order to explain how the human mind has continued to evolve after the human being ceased to evolve, Daniel Dennett thought it necessary to invent a new kind of replicator besides the gene, which accounts for our physiology. He called this new replicator the 'meme' (from *mimesis*, imitation). Memes include human inventions, are embodied in books and can be transmitted by culture. Human consciousness, in Dennett's view, is the product of the evolution of culture by means of the meme. Since he regards the mind as an artefact constructed out of memes, he goes on to compare the mind with a virtual machine, which he says is installed in the computer of the brain.

> Human consciousness is a large complex of memes best understood as the operation of a Neumannesque virtual machine implemented in the parallel architecture of the brain.[6]

The term 'virtual machine' was coined by the designer of the first computer, John von Neumann. A virtual machine is a particular way of operating with signs and bits of matter, such as the pieces of chess. If the same pieces can be used for playing two different kinds of game, either game is a virtual machine. Virtual machines are made of the *rules* for operating the machine rather than of the wires of the computer. According to this analogy, human consciousness is like a programme in a computer. But the mind is not just programmed like a computer, because human beings do not just follow rules in thinking but are able to have spontaneous thoughts and original insights. We are not even like word-processors, for thinking and speaking are not simply a matter of processing words. Man is a *grammatical* being before he is a computing one, since we learn to count and do arithmetic by being taught with words. We need words to say how we are counting and to explain numbers. The ability to discover new meanings in poetry and great literature which may not have been seen by the author is not due to any mechanism in us. If thinking were merely the processing of words, great verse would not contain the variety and depth of meaning that we go on discovering in it. Dennett's theory of the evolution of human consciousness contains just the same sort of gap between the gene and meme, which he says other theories fail to bridge between animal and human consciousness, for he cannot say why a meme should come into existence to begin with.

A further problem with Dennett's theory is that it does not explain how the virtual machine of human consciousness comes to be in the brain when we know that programmes are put into computers by someone else. We cannot explain human consciousness by likening it to a virtual machine when it is just the existence of the virtual machine we need to explain in the first place.

Dennett's explanation of the human mind also fails to explain how we can represent things to ourselves when machines do not. For example, when I look at Van Gogh's picture of the Sunflowers I have a representation of it besides the impression it makes on the retinas of my eyes, but a camera does not have a representation of what it photographs besides the alteration by light of the film. A computer does not represent things to itself. Hilary Putnam has observed that mental states have what he calls a reference to our environment, but computer programmes do not.[7] Our thoughts are directed to things outside us, but what a computer does is not related to anything outside it *for the computer*. It is this very difficulty of materialist theories of mind to explain how we can represent things to ourselves that John Searle takes up. Searle calls the capacity to represent things *intentionality*: intentional states represent objects and states of affairs. Intentionality is the way our thoughts and beliefs are *directed to* objects and states of affairs: for example, a fear of bears, a desire for peace, an opinion about the economy or European union. Intentionality for Searle concerns the way the mind relates to reality.

4. Mental Phenomena

Searle brought back intentionality into the centre of the debate about the mind, because he was dissatisfied with materialist theories that were unable to explain representation. He thought that the reason why many philosophers put forward their materialist theories was a fear that we would be left with dualism unless mental phenomena were reduced to physical ones. By mental phenomena Searle means thoughts, beliefs, hopes, desires, sensations. Searle, however, thinks that mental phenomena cannot be eliminated for the simple reason that when a scientist describes the world or human body, he has some mental phenomena in observing and thinking about what he writes, which are not part of his scientific description of the world. These mental phenomena are irreducible because there would be no scientific account of the world at all unless scientists have them. But Searle sees a need to explain the *cause* of mental phenomena. The trouble with dualism, he thinks, is that it cannot explain how the mind causes the body to act, and with materialism that it deletes mental phenomena as the price of explaining the cause of our actions.

For Searle, causation is simply a matter of one thing making another thing happen in nature. For example, the cause of raising my arm is not just a series of physical processes and reactions but the start of the chain of movement is an *intention*. Perhaps I raise my arm to point to something in the sky. Thus we have to include intention as a cause of our actions, but intention is mental. The question is: how do mental phenomena cause physical actions? Dualism provides a good account of mental phenomena but not of causation; materialism has a good account of causation with some version of the Identity Theory, which makes mental states physical ones. Searle proposes to get right outside the impasse reached in the present debate about the mind by saying that the world contains mental phenomena as it contains physical ones. He seeks a theory that, unlike dualism, can explain how thought causes action but at the same time, unlike materialism, retains mental phenomena. His solution is to say that the world contains mental phenomena like physical ones, but these mental phenomena are features of the physical world: brains are physical but have mental states. Thus thoughts are states of the brain rather than of the mind, but Searle says that they are not physical ones. The world contains physical systems like brains, which have subjective mental states.

Thus Searle sets out to give a *naturalistic* account of intentionality, because unless intention is a part of the natural order we cannot explain how intention causes things in the natural world. Intention is a part of the natural world like any other biological phenomenon: consciousness and intentionality are as much part of human biology as digestion and circulation of the blood, Searle says. 'Mental phenomena are biologically based: they are both caused by operations of the brain and realized in the structure of the brain'.[8] Searle regards mental phenomena as a property of the brain just as being liquid and transparent is a property of water. Water is liquid because molecules of H_2O are in a certain state and liquidity is realized in them, for the liquid state of water is not anything extra besides the molecules of water. In the same way, Searle thinks, intentional states (beliefs and desires) are causal features of the brain, as liquidity is a cause of water. But we would hardly call thought a property of the brain as conductivity is a property of copper wires.

Searle continues his naturalistic theory of intentionality by ascribing its rise to evolution. Intentional phenomena have evolved, he says, because animals too have beliefs, desires and intentions but not the intentional states that go with language; nor do they mean things with words. He thinks that linguistic intentional states have evolved from non-linguistic ones, and that human beings first had intentional states before they had language.[9] This is questionable, since we have not got human nature without language. Searle too readily assumes that human beings are merely continuous with higher animals, although thinking with *concepts* makes human beings different from all other animals. For example, there is no evidence that animals posses a concept like justice. As we do not perceive a gradation from higher animals to humans in the possession of concepts, it seems that our use of concepts cannot be explained by evolution. By talking about consciousness, which animals have in common with us, although they do not have self-consciousness, Searle makes it easier for himself to explain the rise of the human mind from lower forms of consciousness by evolution. As he thinks that we are merely continuous with the rest of nature, he regards language, intelligence and rationality as biological phenomena, which admit a naturalistic explanation.[10] He does not entertain the alternative possibility that, as language, reason and understanding set us apart from all other animals, they may not be biological phenomena that can be explained by evolution. Searle recognizes that one difficulty of treating intentionality as a biological phenomenon is that human thought is *logical*.[11] As intentional states also have a logical structure, they cannot be biological phenomena, because reason (*logos*) distinguishes us from the rest of the biological order. Since we find nothing like logical thoughts in animals, the logical nature of human thought is not just a further stage in the evolution of intentionality from animals but requires another explanation. We cannot explain logic by evolution, because to think logically is to think according to rules of valid reasoning, but doing things by rules is not explained by a theory of evolution, which depends on the movement of matter by chance.

Searle, like van Quine, thinks that all mental phenomena come from 'impacts' on the nervous system and brain. But understanding and ordering the world differ from receiving information about it. Visual experience is caused by the firing of neurons and is realized in the brain, but thinking is not caused like this, because concepts do not come into the brain like impulses along the nerves. It is difficult to see how abstract ideas like constancy and perseverance could come just from impacts on the brain. It is unlikely that the power of understanding has arisen by evolution because it goes in the *opposite* direction to evolution. By evolution things become ever more complex, but greater understanding tends towards seeing things more *simply*.

Searle's explanation of the mind rests on his equating mental with physical phenomena: mental phenomena exist in the world as physical phenomena do.[12] This may be questioned, however, because Searle's claim overlooks that mental phenomena are not quite like physical ones. One sees this when one has the experience of sitting in a medieval building having some thoughts, and asking where were the thoughts three minutes ago and where will my present thoughts and impressions exist in three minutes hence. But the walls around me and the roof above me stood seven hundred years ago and will go on existing long after my mental phenomena have passed. Thus the world does not contain mental phenomena just like the physical phenomena, although thoughts undoubtedly exist in the world; but they are a different kind of thing from the material objects that make up the world. One might also think that if mental states are features of the brain and realized in the brain like liquidity in water, they are really material.

We see that, in order to show that mental phenomena have a physical cause, Searle is led to explain the origin of intentionality by evolution; otherwise, if intentionality cannot be shown to have evolved from matter, one has to seek another cause of the human mind that is characterized by having intentional states.

5 Intentionality

For the Austrian philosopher Franz Brentano (1838-1917), intention is what distinguishes mind from matter. By 'intention' Brentano meant the objects of our thoughts and desires, just as our intention in doing something may also be called our 'object' or aim. Intention comes from *intendere*, the Latin word for to stretch a bow and so to take aim at an object. The first difference between mind and matter for Brentano is that the mind can be related to a content. 'Every psychological phenomenon is characterized by what the Scholastics in the Middle Ages called the intentional (also the mental) inexistence of the object, and what we would call relation to a content, direction upon an object'.[13] Brentano talks about intentional 'inexistence' here, because the objects of our thoughts do not have to exist. Unicorns can still be objects of my thought, although they do not exist in reality. There are objects of thinking and desiring as there are of hitting and pushing, but the objects of thought do not have to exist as the objects of physical actions do. For example I cannot strike an anvil or pull on a shoe that does not exist, but I can think of a crystal sea although no such thing really exists. The mind is related to its object in thinking of it, but the term of the relation (and of the mind's action) does not have to exist as the term of a physical action has to: I am not striking anything if it does not exist, however much I may swing an axe or hammer with my arm.

Brentano's theory of intentionality, however, is not quite like the medieval theory from which he drew it. In the medieval theory, things have their natural and intentional existence. Its natural existence is the way it exists in itself in reality, which for a material object is in some matter. Its intentional existence is the way it exists in the mind of someone thinking of it, which is immaterial. Brentano says that the objects of belief, desire, thought, fear and hope are intentional. These verbs are commonly called 'intentional' verbs today. The object of my fear may be the fall in value of my shares on the Stock Market, although no fall has taken place. Thus the object of my fear does not exist: it has intentional 'inexistence', to use Brentano's expression. Horses with wings can be the object of my thought, although no such things really exist. If the mind, then, can have objects of thought which do not exist, but the objects of physical actions have to exist, the mind cannot be material like matter: what can think of things that do not exist is immaterial. As the objects of physical actions cannot be non-existent, how can the mind be material if it can have non-existent objects of its actions in thinking, desiring etc? The existence of non-material objects naturally has to be explained by any materialist theory of the mind if it is to be adequate.

Nor is it easy to fit free will into a physicalist theory of the mind, for whether you think the movement of particles is determined or random, either way leaves no room for freedom. Either the world is determined, and our wills are also determined by natural motion; or the motion of particles is random, but I do not act by will if my actions are the result of chance movements of matter. As Schrödinger remarks, if all our mental states are bound to physiological processes, their cause will either be determined, so not free, or random, so not voluntary.[14]

In this chapter, we have noted various difficulties of a materialist theory of the mind. For the Identity Theory to work, we will have to be able to correlate mental events with reactions in the brain, but will never be able to do this for self-reflection as well. As scientists cannot completely explain sight by the working of the brain, still less does this approach explain the cause of thought. We cannot explain the mind by comparing it with computers when computers themselves come from minds, which first thought of them. It is difficult to show that intentional thought has a material origin when it cannot be explained like biological phenomena by evolution, because it is also logical. As neither dualism nor materialism provide a complete account of human beings, for dualism overlooks the body and materialism fails to explain the mind, we require a view in-between.

One reason why we need a view that shows the unity of body and soul is so that we can explain the emotions. As the word suggests, in an emotion one thing is moved by another: the body is moved, or affected, by a state of soul. A materialist view does not completely explain the emotions, because they are not just physical states but can be described from various points of view. Aristotle points out that one has not said everything about anger when one has described the rise in blood pressure, because there may also be a reason for being angry, but the physiologist does not include the reason in his account of the symptoms that accompany anger.[15] The emotions neither belong to the soul nor to the body alone, because the soul does not get angry but a human being does, just as we do not say the soul weaves, but a human being.[16] Since dualism cannot explain why the body is affected by the soul if they are separate, but a materialist account does not tell us everything about an emotion, we need a view that keeps the soul with dualism but, unlike dualism, also preserves the unity of a human being. For this we turn to Aristotle's theory of the soul as the form of the body.

NOTES

[1]   *The Elements of Theology* trans. E.R. Dodds (Oxford 1963), Propositions 15 and 186.

[2]   D.M. Armstrong, *A Materialist Theory of Mind* (Routledge & Kegan Paul 1968) 94, 324.

[3]   *The Astonishing Hypothesis* (Simon & Shuster 1994) 22, 24, 209.

[4]   *The New York Review* 8 April 1993, 46.

[5]   *Human Essences*, address to International Conference of Philosophy, Brighton 1998 (unpublished).

[6]   *Consciousness Explained* (Penguin 1991) 210.

[7]   *Representation and Reality* (MIT Massachusetts 1988) 104f.

[8]   *Intentionality* (Cambridge 1983) ix, 15, 264f.

[9]   *Ibid.* 177.

[10] *The Rediscovery of Mind* (Massachusetts 1992) 90.

[11] *Intentionality* 16, 160.

[12] *Ibid.* 271.

[13] *Psychologie vom empirischen Standpunkte II* c.1, 5 (Leipzig 1924) vol. I 124.

[14] *Nature and the Greeks. Science and Humanism* 166.

[15] *De Anima I* c.1 403a 29.

[16] *Ibid. I* c.4 408b 10.

3

ARISTOTLE

Although Aristotle (384-322 B.C.) puts forward a theory of the soul that is regarded as the opposite of dualism, it is worth noting that in the first book of his *De Anima* (On the Soul), in which he reviews what his predecessors thought about the soul, he does not mention Plato. Rather he makes clear that his aim is to refute materialist views of the soul. This should make scholars today pause before they claim his support for their own materialist views by making out that Aristotle was really materialist in his conception of the soul or that he was more interested in sensation and imagination than he was in intellect. The general conception of the soul before him, he says, was that it is 'the principle of movement and perception'.[1] Aristotle notes that materialists before him thought that the soul consisted of one of the elements because of the principle 'like is known by like'. He asks why does not every material thing have a soul if the soul is composed of matter, and how could the soul know that something is a man or a mineral, which is to know its form, if it were material. Aristotle concluded that, as we discern the forms of things, the soul is not composed of material elements but is itself a *form*. The soul is a form, because it knows the forms of things.

The soul is the form of a living body for Aristotle, because it is the 'first actuality of a body with potential for life'.[2] Matter by itself, according to Aristotle, is purely potential: matter is only found existing with some definite form. The form is what makes it be matter of some kind and thus gives it actual existence. The soul is the form of the body because it makes it a living body. Not any kind of matter can be the matter of a living body but only matter with a certain structure that can carry life: thus matter 'with potential for life'. Although we may find Aristotle's definition of the soul as the '*actuality*' of a living body not very helpful at first sight, a 20th century scientist who thought that life could be explained by chemistry, has defined life in terms remarkably similar to Aristotle's definition of the soul. For J.D. Bernal wrote: 'Life is a partial, continuous, progressive, multiform and conditionally active, self-realization of the potentialities of atomic electron states'.[3] When we reduce this lengthy expression to its main constituents, we see that 'realization' corresponds with Aristotle's actuality (and is perhaps a better translation of *entelecheia* than 'actuality'); 'potentialities of atomic electron states' is equivalent to the potential of matter (for life). The word *entelecheia* suggests that the soul completes the body (*telos* means an end in Greek).

Aristotle explains what he means by calling the soul the form of the body with the help of an analogy. Suppose, he says, there were a living thing that was just an eye; then sight would be its soul. If there were such a thing, it would have only one activity, that of seeing, and it would be by this activity alone that it was alive. Aristotle says that the eye is matter for sight and sight is what makes the matter of the eye able to see. Sight realizes the potential of this matter for seeing. He then says that, as the eye is matter with potential for sight and sight is what makes this matter actually see, so a body is matter with potential for life and the soul is what makes it actually live. As the matter of an eye and sight constitute an eye, so body and soul together make an animal.[4]

For Aristotle, then, the primary aspect of the soul is that it makes something *live*. This is quite different from the modern conception of the soul, which ever since Descartes has primarily been associated with *consciousness*. As we saw, Descartes divided the world into conscious and unconscious things or substances. But Aristotle came to his conception of the soul by observing that some things in the world are living and other things non-living. In this way we do not start talking about the soul by introspection, as Descartes did, but by looking outwards at the visible world and, like Aristotle, asking what is it that all living things have in common which distinguishes them from all non-living things. Aristotle thought that this must be what he called a primary principle of life. This is the soul. The soul is not just *a* principle of life but the *primary* principle of life, because various parts of the body like the heart, lungs and brain might be called principles of life in that the basic living activities depend on them; but before these organs appear the organism is *already* alive; its life is continuous with the life it first has when it begins as an independent unit before the appearance of any of its organs.

Life, Aristotle notes, is *manifest in activity*. Aristotle distinguished the following five basic forms of living activity. First comes growth and reproduction. With growth also goes decay. All living things have these two powers. No kind of living thing is without the power to reproduce its kind, or else the species would die out after only one generation. Then comes the power of self-movement and sensation. A stick cannot move itself unless moved by something else but a hedgehog can. Things that can move themselves need to know where they are going so that they can protect themselves and avoid harm; thus they are equipped with the senses for knowing the world around them. The fifth and highest power is reason and understanding. Plants only have the first two powers. Animals also have the next two powers. The final power distinguishes human beings from all other animals. These five basic kinds of activity spring from powers of the soul. Souls with different kinds of power are different kinds of soul. Thus plants have vegetative souls, animals sensitive souls and human beings rational souls. But animals do not have two kinds of soul because they have sensation as well as the powers of plants, nor human beings three souls, but a higher kind of soul includes the powers of a lower kind of soul, so that each living thing has only one soul, for every thing has only one *substantial* form, which makes it be the kind of thing it is.

How the primary principle of life, the soul, is the form of a living thing can be seen in four ways: the growth of living

things, their unity, their identity and what happens when they
die.

Growth

One way we see that the soul is the form of the body is by
comparing living with artificial things. Living things grow by
their own power, artefacts are made by an external agent. An
artefact is formed out of already formed parts, which are put
together. The parts exist before the whole; the whole only gets its
form at the *end* of the process of making it. A machine with the
form of a bicycle, for example, only exists when all its parts have
been put together. But a living organism exists *before* its parts
appear. A zygote does not unfold like a Japanese flower, with all
its parts preformed in miniature, but is already a living unit. It
seems to possess its form from the beginning of its existence
before it has reached its completed growth. We see why a living
thing grows by its form that it has from the beginning when we
consider why an acorn, which looks very different from an oak
tree, grows into something with the same form as produced it:
another oak tree. Thus it seems to grow by its form, which makes
it alive. Reproduction is anyway of a thing's form rather than its
matter: a living thing reproduces itself by producing something
that grows with the same form but the matter is added. This
power to reproduce itself distinguishes a living thing from an
artefact. When you put a post into the ground it does not grow
into a tree, but when you put a cutting from a geranium into a
pot it grows into a new geranium.

Unity

An artefact is made *out of* its parts, but the parts of a living thing
grow out of it. A living thing has a *unity*, because it grows out of
a single cell. A sewing machine, for example, is made by adding
one part *to* another, but a living thing grows *out of* the unit it
begins as. Thus a machine is an *assemblage* of parts, which can
be dismantled and re-assembled, but we are not an assemblage
of parts, because the parts of us have an *essential* unity. The parts
of a watch, for example, only have an accidental unity, because

when you take the watch to pieces each of its parts continues to exist on its own with the form of a wheel, or of a spindle, or of a spring, etc. But you cannot take a living thing apart like this and then put its parts together again, because it is a unity. When an arm is amputated it does not remain a human arm on its own but only when united with its body. When amputated, an arm quickly loses its visible form unless it is preserved by *artificial means*. The same applies to all the other parts of the body.

This leads us to another remarkable power of living bodies. When they absorb nourishment, which is by matter being added to the body, the new matter is converted into something *with the same form* as the thing that receives it. But when you mix quantities of non-living matter, say tin and copper, with one another, you get matter with a different form from either of them, a third, new thing, namely pewter, resulting from them. Thus living bodies, including plants, have the power to convert the matter of their nourishment into something with their own form. For example, vegetable is converted into a body with the human or the ox form. It is by doing this that they grow; we suggested above that living things grow by their form.

Sir Charles Sherrington, a neurophysiologist, asked why a body has a *unified* life when it consists of countless cells, each of which is a unit of life.[5] We might think that, since a living body gets its unity from its form, for, unlike an artefact, it is not just an assemblage of parts but has an essential unity, it also has a unified life because of its form. Although we ascribe its various powers, such as seeing, respiring and digesting, to different parts of the body, they can only exercise their powers as parts of the living whole. Thus the structure of the parts of the body does not by itself explain its living activities. As the parts only function when they are parts of a unified living body, so their powers are explained by what gives the living body its unity, which is its form, the soul. Seeing, for example, is done through the eye but an eye does not see: an animal sees with its eyes. The eye is an instrument of seeing. ('Organ' comes from '*organon*', the Greek word for an instrument.) Aristotle called the hand 'an organ of organs', because only human beings can make and use instruments. A beaver cuts wood with its teeth but we with a saw.

Identity

The third way we see that the soul is the form of a living body is the way it has its Identity Theory. The identity of a living body differs from that of an artefact. The identity of a living thing is not the identity of its matter, for its matter continually changes. Yet a living thing persists as the same individual through all the changes of its matter. So the identity of a living thing consists of something else - its form. The identity of an artefact, for example of a spade, consists in it being the same pieces of wood and metal. Although all the matter of a living body is renewed (this happens every seven years in a human body), the body remains the same body. The body of an old person is identical with the body he or she had as a child. It is continuous with the body he or she had at any previous stage of life. It does not have material but *numerical* identity, for the body is never changed for a new one but only its matter is continually replaced, bit by bit, by new matter. A living body is like a river: matter flows through the body as water through a river.[6] Although ever fresh water enters into the river and passes down it into the sea, the river remains the same river. As water flows through a river, so a living body consists of matter flowing through a certain form. It is the same form which gives a living body its identity: its form is what makes it alive, its soul, which gives the body its unity. A living thing has the same form throughout its life, which makes it alive.

Another difference between a living body and an artefact is that a living body only exists as long as it has some activity, at least of metabolism or photosynthesis (if it is a plant). For living things to exist is for them to be alive (*viventibus esse est vivere*), and nothing is alive without being active in some way. But a spade or a tractor remains the same instrument or machine when it stands still and is inactive. Not that a spade has any activity of its own, properly speaking, for it only digs when it is moved by someone living. The same is true of a mechanical digger: it needs to be set in motion and guided by a living person. A spade keeps its form when it is not being used and is inert, but a living thing only keeps its form as long as it is alive. To be alive is to be active in some way.

Dead Matter

We also see that what makes something alive, its primary principle of life, is its form when we consider what happens to it when it dies. The primary principle of life is the form of a living thing, because it visibly loses its form when it loses its principle of life. Thus what gives a body its form is what makes it alive. Although the corpse of a human being seems to have the human form, because it still looks like a human being, it has lost its form because it cannot preserve its outward form, or shape, by itself. Also whatever has the human form is a human being, but a corpse is not a human being because it does not have the activities of a human being. Indeed the matter of a dead body has no activity of its own but is rather *acted upon* by external agents, which dissolve it, as it disintegrates and decays. The soul gives the body its unity because, when it loses its principle of life, its loses its unity. A dead body does not, properly speaking, have a form of any definite kind. Whatever else a corpse may be, it is not a human being; it no longer belongs to the human race. Rather it *was* a human being. This truth is brought out for us by Shakespeare in the natural way we speak when Hamlet, in the Grave Digger's scene (Act V scene 1) asks: 'What man dost thou dig it for?' and receives the reply, 'For no man, sir, nor woman either' but for 'One that was a woman, sir' (referring to Ophelia). We could emphasize the 'was' here.

One could object that when we see stuffed birds in a museum, we still call them parrots or owls or eagles or whatever kind of bird they were. We might think that what still looks like a parrot has the form of a parrot, but we would hardly think that something with straw inside it and glass eyes has the same form as a living parrot. A living thing is able to preserve its form, but a dead body cannot be preserved except artificially. A stuffed parrot once was a parrot. A parrot is a kind of animal but a carcass is not an animal. Nor does a corpse have the form of a human being.

Properties of life

Some people today hold that what makes a body live is not the soul but certain properties of a living body. According to this opinion, a body grows, moves, is conscious, perceives and, if a human being, thinks because it has certain vital properties which enable it to do these things. This view may well go with saying that a living body consists of its chemical constituents and living properties, together with principles of organization and powers of growth. When people with this view are pressed to name these properties, they come out with a list that is almost the same as the powers of soul which Aristotle distinguished: growth, reproduction, movement, perception and understanding.

Although it is common to regard the soul as the organization of a body with powers of life, the soul is not the organization of the parts of a body in the same way as the form of a house may be called the organization of the parts of a house: bricks, timbers, windows, floors etc. The form of a house does not give its parts their form, because the bricks and timbers already exist as bricks and timbers before they are used for building a house. But the parts of a body only exist as parts of a living body. They neither precede the body, nor exist on their own when separated from the body. This is because, as we have already noted, living things have an *essential* unity - but artefacts only have accidental unity. A thumb only has its form as long as it is a living thumb. The parts of a body only have life when they have the form of the whole body. One difficulty of the view that what we mean by the soul is the properties of a living body is how to give an account of what *unites* the properties, since it is clear that every living organism has a unity. The simplest explanation of this is that the powers of a living body are united because they flow from a *single principle*, which is its soul.

To think that a living body is no more than a body with certain properties of life makes the power of thinking and understanding a property of the body too. Thus it implies a materialist view of the mind. But if you do not think that thought is a property of the body, it must be the property or power of something else.

In this chapter, I have tried to make intelligible Aristotle's theory that the form of a living body is its soul. We began by noting that what distinguishes living from non-living things is a primary principle of life. This primary principle of life is the form of a living thing because of the way it grows and is formed. Unlike the artefacts we make, which only get their form at the end of their making, living things already have their form before their parts appear, because they have one continuous life from the start. This form explains the unity of a living body, which is an essential unity, because the parts only have their form as long as they are parts of the living body. The form also explains the identity of a living thing, because this is not the identity of its matter, which is always changing; so it is of its form. Finally, when a body loses its principle of life and dies, it loses its form, as can be seen quite visibly. One could, however, say that we no longer need the soul to explain the life, growth, unity and identity of a living thing, because its life can be explained in a scientific and purely material way. Before we continue our inquiry into the soul, then, we must next consider the view of many scientists today, that we can explain the rise of life from matter by evolution.

NOTES

1   *De Anima I* c.2 403b 27.

2   *Ibid. II* c.1 412a 28.

3   *The Origin of Life* (Weidenfeld & Nicholson 1967) 168.

4   *De Anima II* c.1 412b 18.

5   *Man and his Nature* (Cambridge 1953) 66.

6   G.E.M. Anscombe, *Three Philosophers* (Blackwell 1967) 56. The analogy comes from Aristotle, *De Generatione et Corruptione I* c.5, 322a 24.

4

EVOLUTION

The theory of evolution is meant to explain how higher forms of life have developed from simpler ones by the random mutation of genes, and how the first living things originally arose from lifeless matter purely by chemical processes. The theory of evolution is not the same as that of natural selection. Natural selection explains why some variations of species survived rather than others, but it does not tell us why the variations occurred in the first place. Natural selection is a part of the theory of evolution. The theory of evolution is that the variety of plant and animal species is the result of higher animals developing from lower ones by a process that began with the spontaneous movement of matter. Since plants and animals consist of living cells, the first thing that the theory of evolution has to explain is the origin of life itself. Just as an animal comes from an animal, and a plant from a plant, so a living cell comes from a living cell. This was stated as an axiom by the German biologist, Rudolf Virchow (1821-1902): 'Where a cell arises, there a cell must have preceded it'. But this does not account for the first living cell in the chain of living things: either it came from non-living matter or the first unit of life had some other cause than matter.

The Primal Soup

Let us first consider the possibility that living cells originally came from non-living matter. The best known theory for this is that life arose in a 'primal soup', which coalesced in the ocean.

A typical description of this theory is given by the psychologist, Nicholas Humphrey:

> In the primal soup, chance brought together the first molecules of life, with the capacity to generate new copies of themselves. Time passed and Darwinian evolution got to work, selecting - and hence helping to design - packets of world stuff with ever greater potential for maintaining their own integrity and reproducing. First there were just complex living molecules (like DNA), then single cells (like bacteria and amoebae), then multicelled organisms (like worms, or fish, or us).[1]

We may notice a number of points about this passage. First, it does not tell us how molecules of life came into existence, except that it was by chance; but this is the very thing that needs explaining. Secondly, Humphrey assumes the existence of something called 'Darwinian evolution', which he introduces as a personified force or agent. Thirdly, he supposes that the molecules of life have the capacity to generate new copies of themselves, which they may well have had, but this cannot be explained by his theory, for it requires an already complex mechanism working for an end. But he has said that 'the first molecules were brought together by chance' (an end does not come about by chance). Fourthly, Humphrey assumes that DNA existed on its own at first, although it has never been shown that this was possible, because DNA only works as part of a living organism, so cannot be invoked to explain the genesis of the first living organisms. Finally, Humphrey permits himself to say that Darwinian evolution 'designs' packets of world stuff (whatever the vague expression 'world stuff' may mean). But what designs things does not act by chance, because to design something presupposes having a *conception* of what is to be produced. A conception requires a designer, which is the very thing that the theory of evolution is meant to render unnecessary: the process of evolution replaces a designer in a materialist theory of evolution.

Let us now look at some of the scientific attempts to show that it was possible for molecules of life to have originated from non-living matter in a primal soup. In the 1920's a Russian scientist, Oparin, conducted experiments to create the conditions in which life could have arisen by passing light through a mixture of hydrogen, ammonia and methane. J.B.S. Haldane said that a primal soup could have been formed in the oceans, because ultra-violet rays act on a mixture of water, carbon-dioxide and ammonia to form organic substances like sugars and some materials of proteins. He thought that the first molecules were synthesized by the sun's radiation, but said that highly specialized molecules were required before they could reproduce themselves. He admitted that the hypothesis that life originated from inanimate matter by itself remains unproven as long as no one has succeeded in producing life or synthesizing a living cell in a laboratory, which no scientist has done so far.[2] Professor Steven Rose reports no significant advance in attempts to produce life from non-living matter in the revised edition of his book, *The Chemistry of Life*, in 1999.

In 1953, Oparin's theory was put to the test by the American, Stanley Miller, who passed electric sparks through a mixture of methane, ammonia, molecular hydrogen and water. He found that conditions suitable for the rise of life must have already been complex. It was then recognized that the gap between non-living and living matter was greater than had first been supposed. In the 1980's, the Nobel Prize winner Max Delbrück wrote: 'By contrast, a vast gulf separates all creatures, large and small, from inanimate matter, a gulf that seems much wider today than it seemed a few decades ago.'[3] Thus attempts to synthesize life, far from bringing us closer to producing life from non-living matter by scientific experiment, have only made clearer the difficulty of explaining life in terms of chemistry alone. At about the same time, Freeman Dyson said that we have no evidence for the transition from a lifeless organic soup to organized biological metabolism.[4] He though that scientists had to go beyond the evidence of experiments to 'theory' in order to explain the origin of life.

One difference between molecules of inanimate matter, like stone, and a living cell is that a cell is 1) organized, 2) has the power to convert the matter it absorbs into energy, 3) stores information, which controls its living processes, and 4) has a mechanism for duplicating itself accurately. Thus a living cell does not just have a structure like a crystal but also a complex *function*. Having a function, or purpose, cannot be explained by blind matter or by chance.

Even if the origin of life could be explained by natural science, all theories of evolution would still face the difficulty of explaining how the first cells which could replicate themselves came into existence. Steven Rose says that the probability of highly complex molecular structures being assembled by chance is so slender that it may be regarded as impossible.[5] No living species survives more than one generation unless it can reproduce itself. How is it possible to explain the rise of the complex from the simple when the means of reproducing must itself already be complex from the start? One way of getting round this difficulty is to suppose, like Dyson, that there was a double origin of life. At first there were cells which only had metabolism and continued by dividing. These cells were later invaded by others with a replicating system. This sort of solution, however, only pushes the difficulty elsewhere, perhaps to some extraterrestrial source, for the origin of these replicating cells likewise needs to be explained.

If, as is supposed, life arose from a series of chemical reactions by chance, the molecules from which the first living cells came also developed by chance. But for living cells to have appeared when molecules reached a certain complexity, the molecules must have had an *aim*, which is contrary to happening by chance, since the division of cells proceeds towards a definite *end*: the formation of a complete organism. Cells need 'instructions' written into their genetic material, in order to grow into a definite kind of living thing. There is nothing living which does not belong to a definite species. But instructions do not get written by chance, since instructions have an *intention*. The first living organisms cannot have arisen by chance, because their material constituents have a pattern, but order is contrary to random movement. Things are *directed* to their end.

Another possibility is that, before there were any living organisms, there were molecules which could replicate themselves. But molecules of DNA would still have had to have the characteristics of a definite species to produce living organisms, otherwise the organisms would not have survived. A system of replicating has to work precisely if it is to produce viable life, otherwise errors multiply, the species degenerates and fails. But working precisely excludes coming about by chance. This theory also assumes that DNA existed on its own in the transition from inanimate matter to the first living organism. But DNA has never been found surviving on its own outside an organism. As noted above, it requires the machinery of a living body in order to be an active cause of replication.

Dawkins

This difficulty was admitted by Richard Dawkins in explaining the first step in evolution. Drawing an analogy with Xerox machines, he has said that molecules of DNA replicate in the complex machinery of the cell as written words are replicated in a copying machine, but neither molecules nor words replicate themselves without some machinery to support them.[6] Dawkins' analogy argues against the existence of pieces of DNA on their own before there were any living organisms. Although his explicit aim is to explain how complex things arose from simple ones, he has to presuppose the existence of complicated machinery for the origin of the simplest living organisms.

Dawkins supposes, 'There must somehow, as a consequence of the ordinary laws of physics, come into being *self-copying* entities or, as I shall call them, *replicators*'.[7] Since, however, the laws of physics explain the order and coherence of the universe, they cannot be used to explain something that is supposed to have happened by chance. Dawkins assumes the laws of physics but overlooks that they too require an explanation, because stable laws do not come from chance. As a biologist, he is quite at liberty to say that he does not need to provide any explanation of them, but as his theory of evolution presupposes them, he cannot also claim to explain the cause of the universe. According to Dawkins, the universe is not the work of a

Designer. This is quite at variance with his own criterion for a well designed organism: that it includes all the components an intelligent mechanic would give it for performing some activity well, such as wings for flying or lenses that adjust themselves to the strength of light.[8] He seems not to admit that, if things in nature are well designed when they have the mechanisms an intelligent mechanic would give them, then a world full of living things with well designed organs may also have an intelligent designer.

Dawkins believes that the living species have evolved by 'cumulative selection'. He has to allow that cumulative selection is not random in its result, because there obviously is order in nature, although he says that it proceeds by chance mutations. If every step in the series occurs by chance, however, the end cannot be ordered. To advance to anywhere requires having a destination before you set out. If every step on the route may be taken in any direction, once you diverge from the path to the goal you only go further off-course by continuing in that direction. The only way of getting back to the path that leads to the end is to correct your course, but you can only correct it by having a destination or end. Dawkins thinks that you can explain how random movement may produce an ordered result by the way that the sea washes up pebbles on to the beach, but they are left in an ordered series of shelves with the heaviest lowest down the beach and the lightest at the top. Although the throwing up of the pebbles may look random, the laws of physics are at work as the pebbles settle at different levels according to their weight. This example does not explain how order is reached by random steps in cumulative selection unless the laws of physics, which Dawkins pre-supposes here, are also explained, for they did not come into existence by chance.

The vast array of plant and animal species, Dawkins thinks, can be explained as the working out of the possible mathematical variations of a simple shape by a computer. For his original shape Dawkins selects a Y, which can be recognized in the swallow-tail butterfly, the head of a fox (eyes and nose), the flower of a bee-orchid, and in a beetle. Dawkins supposes that evolution could have worked in the same way as a computer 'evolves' the variations of a primary shape. To talk about computers 'evolving' variations of a design is to use an analogy with nature; so it cannot be used to explain how nature works. Secondly, the computer cannot evolve variations altogether of itself, for it requires someone to provide it with the original pattern. Dawkins admits that he has to give his computer a programme to do this in the first place. As he frequently uses the analogy of computers to make his theory of evolution plausible, he should draw the conclusion that, if nature acts like the programme of a computer, nature too is not blind but, like computers, comes from an intelligent designer.

One may well ask why the variations by which species have evolved, one from another, occurred in the first place. A leading advocate of the theory of evolution today, Mark Ridley, notes that there has been a great advance in the understanding of natural selection but little progress in explaining variation itself, why it happens at all.[9] Natural selection does not produce the variation but only explains the course of the variations once they have been produced, by the survival of the stronger and elimination of the weaker strains. Some things in nature happen by chance, such as the carrying of seeds by the wind, but the growth of living things cannot be explained in this way, because it proceeds to an *end*, which is contrary to things occurring at random. The living species have not come about by chance, for 'by chance nothing comes about with any aim'. In contrast with Dawkins, the mathematician and physicist, Roger Penrose, sees an intelligent directing in the course of evolution. 'Things at least *seem* to organize themselves somewhat better than they 'ought' to, just on the basis of blind-chance evolution and natural selection.'[10]

The Chemistry of Life

The theory that life arose from inanimate matter by chance makes us ask how molecules with the genetic information, or instructions, required for developing into a definite kind of organism came of their own accord from compounds of chemicals. Chemistry explains how cells divide but it does not tell us why they are living. If it could do this, it would be possible for us to construct living cells. But it is not possible for chemists even to construct wood. If life were merely a matter of chemistry, we would only need to discover the chemical formula of life and we would be able to synthesize living matter. Although scientists have now unraveled the chemical constitution of DNA, which might be thought to contain the source of life if any matter does, we are still unable to make living things out of inanimate matter. Although the eye is like a camera, we can make a camera to record images but not an eye out of the constituents of matter, the salt, water and albumen, that make up an eye.

Even if we could construct all the parts of a goldfish or a flower, it is doubtful whether we could make a *living* goldfish or flower. If we could manufacture things that were not just mechanical goldfish or flowers but fish that swam and flowers that unfolded their petals, we would be creating life. One reason why we cannot do this is that living things are not formed like artificial ones. We manufacture artefacts by putting together parts, but living things grow out of a single unit, as we saw in the previous chapter. Biologists can put together bits of matter but a living thing develops out of a single cell. We begin making things with many parts, a living thing begins as one. Thus living things are not like machines and do not grow mechanically.

J. Arthur Thomson said that there is no mechanistic explanation of the way a chicken egg develops. An embryo is not formed like a new constellation of stars out of an amorphous blob of matter, because it does not turn into any shape, like clouds, but has the same form as the thing it came from. This made Thomson declare that life is not just a matter of physics and chemistry.[11] Arthur Peacocke points out that physics and chemistry do not explain a machine, because the configuration of its parts do not merely derive from the properties of the materials used to make it. This is even more true of living cells: they are not explained by the properties of their matter.[12] Peacocke concludes that physics and chemistry do not explain the emergence of new forms of organized matter any more than the properties of copper and iron explain the appearance of the steam engine. We may point out that what explains the rise of the steam engine is the mind that designed it. In view of the difficulties of explaining life purely in terms of physics and chemistry, we should be open to the view that life does not have a purely material explanation but its source is something other than matter alone. This was the view of Alfred Russell Wallace (1823-1913).

Some New Cause

Although Wallace was keen to promote the theory of natural selection, which he may have worked out independently at the same time as Darwin, he thought that evolution could not explain its three decisive stages: the origin of life itself, the rise of sensation and consciousness, which separates the animal from the plant kingdom, and the intellect that separates man from the rest of animals. 'There are at least three stages in the development of the organic world when some new cause or power must necessarily have come into action'.[13] We should note that Wallace's three decisive stages in evolution correspond exactly with Aristotle's three kinds of soul: vegetative, sensitive, and intellective. Wallace did not just suppose 'some new cause or power' for the rise of the human mind but for all three decisive steps in the course of evolution: from inanimate to animate matter, from life to sensation, and from sensation to thinking. In particular, Wallace questioned whether the higher-order consciousness of human beings could have evolved from the lower-order consciousness of other animals. To be conscious is to be *aware* of other things and have sensation. The difference between lower and higher order consciousness is that higher-order consciousness includes being conscious of one's consciousness or, as Bertrand Russell put it, not merely being acquainted with other things but being acquainted with one's acquaintance: 'animals we may suppose, though they have acquaintance with sense-data, never become aware of this acquaintance and thus never know of their own existence'.[14]

Although Wallace was convinced that plants and animals perpetually vary and the useful variations are preserved in the struggle for survival, he did not think that natural selection explains the intellectual abilities of human beings, since superior

intelligence has not always proved successful over force in the
fight for existence. The Romans were overcome by barbarian
races. The variation of intellectual ability among human beings
is far greater than the variation between any two species next to
one another. Evolution cannot account for the leap in the ability
to do mathematics from primitive tribes to Archimedes and
Newton, because this leap occurred in a short space of time but
the theory of evolution requires only very slight changes over
a long period of time. Each change can only be slight because
living things cannot produce any offspring markedly different
from themselves. The variation in intelligence, Wallace says,
'compels us to recognize some origin wholly distinct from that
which has served to account for the animal characteristics of
man'.[15] He did not think that the rise of human intelligence can
be explained in the same way as our physiology, by evolution,
but that the intellect has another productive cause than the
body: 'some other influence, law or agency is required to
account for them (our intellectual abilities)'.[16] Wallace thought
it was out of the question that a mere complication of structure
could have produced sensation or consciousness, let alone the
human mind.

But can even the rise of primary consciousness and
sensation be explained by evolution? On the one hand, it
seems quite possible that living organisms became conscious
when they acquired sufficiently complex organs for having
sensation. Above all, consciousness would have first appeared
with the evolution of a nervous system; without this there can
be no sensation. On the other hand, although consciousness
depends on a nervous system, one might think that it was no
more possible for some living matter to become conscious for
the first time than it was for non-living matter to produce life.
In other words, there is the same sort of gap between non-
conscious and conscious life as between inanimate and animate
matter, and the same difficulty about explaining the appearance
of consciousness as there is about the rise of life.

Even if we grant that the theory of evolution can explain
the second decisive stage in evolution, the rise of consciousness
(although it cannot yet explain the first, the rise of life), it

cannot explain the rise of the mind merely by the evolution of a sufficiently complex brain. C.S. Lewis did not think it possible to explain the human mind by evolution, because there is an unbridgeable gap between sensation and reasoning. No amount of improvement of the *organ* of sight, he observes, brings us any nearer to *knowledge* of what light is. Knowing what light is is not just a matter of being able to see more clearly. Rather this knowledge was discovered by Newton and others by *reasoning* about the phenomena of light they observed in experiments.[17] Thus our ability to know is not just due to the evolution of more complex organs.

The case of thinking that we can explain the mind as just a further step in the evolution of consciousness is that consciousness clearly has a physiological basis. I cannot think unless I am conscious and I am not conscious unless my brain is in a certain physical state, for example, not anaesthetized or heavily intoxicated by alcohol. The brain needs to be in a suitable physical state, because we require the data that are transmitted to the brain in order to have something to think on. But just because we need the brain for thinking does not mean that the brain explains thinking. Human consciousness differs from lower-order consciousness in several respects. Even when we have explained sensation and imagination, which may be regarded as material, because we receive images through the senses that have bodily organs, we still have not explained the ability to think with concepts, which are abstract and so immaterial. Thinking with concepts is more than thinking with images. Thinking about colours, for example having the concept of a primary colour, differs from just distinguishing colours. We noted in the second chapter that human beings are also distinguished from other animals by self-reflection, which is not material, and by the power to think *logically*. But thinking according to laws of reasoning does not come from evolution by chance. These differences suggest that the human mind is not explained by evolution, because it is not merely continuous with the consciousness of animals.

In this chapter, I have noted that, since all living things consist of cells, the theory of evolution needs to explain the origin of the first living cell. But no scientist has so far been able to show that life arose from non-living matter by itself. Another difficulty in explaining the rise of life in a purely material way is that evolution presupposes the existence of a complex mechanism for reproduction at the beginning. Evolution by chance does not explain the development of replicating cells, which have instructions. The life of things seems to be more than the sum of its material constituents, so that it is not just explained by chemistry. Wallace thought that all three decisive stages of evolution, not just the rise of intelligence, required some new cause or power. Although his name is little mentioned today, this may not be because his view lacks merit but because it is inconvenient for the dominant view of scientists today. We now go on to consider, in the next chapter, whether a materialist theory of evolution could explain the advent of the mind.

NOTES

1   *A History of Mind* (London 1993) 17.
2   The Origin of Life (1929), in *On Being the Right Size* (Oxford 1985) 111.
3   *Mind from Matter* (Blackwell 1986) 270.
4   *Origins of Life* (Cambridge 1985) 30.
5   *The Chemistry of Life* (Penguin 1999) 361.
6   *The Blind Watchmaker* (Penguin 1988) 140.
7   *Ibid.* 128.
8   *Ibid.* 19.
9   *The Problems of Evolution* (Oxford 1985) 43.
10   *The Emperor's New Mind* (Vintage 1990) 538.
11   *The System of Animate Nature* (London 1920) vol. I 117.
12   *Science and the Christian Experiment* (Oxford 1971) 85.
13   *Darwinism* (Macmillan 1890) 474.
14   *The Problems of Philosophy* (1912 Oxford 1967) 27.
15   *Darwinism* 473.
16   *Ibid.* 463.
17   *Miracles* (1947 Collins 1974) 23.

5

THE MIND

There are two main theories of the mind. One is that it is something subsistent, the other that it is a bundle of perceptions or complex of mental states. Some, like the American philosopher van Quine, also call it a net of beliefs. Most of those who deny that the mind is anything subsistent adopt the second view. This view comes from the Scottish philosopher, David Hume (1711-1776), who said that the mind is a bundle of perceptions. Perceptions include impressions and ideas for Hume.

Hume did not believe in the idea of substance, because we have no impression of it, he says. All ideas are derived from impressions for Hume. As we have no idea of an external substance distinct from the ideas of its particular qualities, he says, so we have no notion of the mind distinct from its perceptions.[1] As we can conceive perceptions distinctly, so they do not need anything to inhere in but can exist by themselves. Thus Hume makes the mind identical with its perceptions: what we mean by the mind is our thoughts and perceptions.

This view of the mind has various disadvantages. If the mind were identical with its perceptions, it would subsist in them rather than they inhere in it. Also we would have no mind before we had perceptions and thoughts. This would be like saying that we do not possess the power of sight before we see. As the reason why we see for the first time is because we already possess the power of sight, so the reason why we think is because we have the power of the mind *before* we have thoughts and perceptions. The mind does not just consist in its thoughts but, to use a word of Hume's, thoughts *actuate* the power of the mind.

If the mind is identical with its perceptions but is not always having perceptions, it has no continuous existence or, therefore, identity. As the mind is not always thinking, we need to have the idea of the mind as a *power* of something. Hume saw no need to think of the mind as a power, since he saw little difference between power and action; 'I begin by observing that the terms of *efficacy*, *agency*, power ... are all nearly synonymous'.[2] We need to distinguish between power and action, however, since we still retain a power even when not using it, and the reason why we are able to perform certain activities is because we have the power to do them. As Aristotle remarks, we do not acquire hearing from acts of hearing but we hear because we first have the power to hear.[3] Likewise, we do not acquire a mind by thinking but an infant has it first thoughts because it *already* possesses the power of the mind. As a child already has this power, or capacity, before it actually thinks, it seems that we cannot say when it is first present. This is a question which will be discussed more fully in chapter seven. But, if the mind were identical with its thoughts, having a mind would be the consequence of having thoughts rather than the reason why we have them.

Another disadvantage of the theory is that, if the mind were just its thoughts, it could not reflect on them; we would not have self-reflection. In order to turn to its thoughts and reflect on them, our mind must be something else besides it thoughts or contents. If it is just its thoughts, it cannot turn to these thoughts, for the thought about these thoughts cannot just be one of them. The first thing to be said about the view that the mind is identical with its contents is that things are only contents because they are *contained* by something. For example, a collection of buttons is not the contents of anything unless it is the contents of a box or basket; otherwise, the buttons are just a lot of separate buttons with nothing to unite them.

Not surprisingly, Hume had a difficulty in explaining the unity of our thoughts and so our identity. As the mind is identical with its perceptions for him, he says that perceptions constitute the self, because whenever I look into myself I never catch myself without a perception. To have an idea of myself however, it needs to be the same idea for Hume. But I do not have a constant idea of myself, because every time that I look into myself I catch myself with a different perception. Hume acknowledges this difficulty in the Appendix he published with Book I of his *Treatise of Human Nature* in 1740. He found himself caught in a dilemma, wanting to hold together two key principles of his thought, which are inconsistent with one another. On the one hand, he needs to explain the unity of our perceptions but he does not think that we can discern the real connection between things. On the other hand, he holds that the mind is identical with its perceptions, although he cannot show they belong to the same mind if it is not possible to see any real connection between them. He resolves his dilemma by resorting to his famous principle of the association of ideas: we associate ideas either because they resemble one another, or because they come next to one another, or because they have the relation of cause and effect as one thought leads to another.

Thus the mind is something more than just its thoughts if we are to be able to explain the unity of our thoughts and the power to think. We see that the mind is an *active* power, that is, something able to *produce* thoughts, in the following way. We know from experiments that animals are able to distinguish between objects of different shapes because they respond to them differently. But for all that they are not able to do geometry, which involves having concepts like area, diagonal, angle, bisect. An animal apprehends shapes with the imagination, but understanding is different from imagination: the understanding sees the relations between shapes. An animal may distinguish between a circle and a triangle, but you will not get an animal to see that a cone is circular and triangular in shape together. Nor do animals construct new figures from the shapes they are presented with, as we can. We are able to *do* things with geometrical shapes, make new ones out of them, see the proofs for their properties, such as that the angles of a triangle are equal to two right angles. This means that the human mind is an active power; thoughts do not just occur to us, but we also *produce* them.

If the mind is a power, as I have argued above, it must be the power of something. I now want to argue that it is not the power of anything material by considering concepts, numbers, understanding and self-reflection.

Concepts

Every material thing is particular in its existence. Every flower is a particular kind of flower: it is a rose or a snowdrop or a delphinium. But I also have the concept of a flower, which covers all flowers. It is having the concept of a flower that enables me to recognize anything as a flower. The concept is general. Likewise, every hat has a particular size and shape, but the concept of hat fits all hats. My concept of a coin fits coins of every size, metal and value. A concept is not like a mental image, which is of an individual thing. The difference between a concept and a mental image is well brought out by Elizabeth Anscombe with the following illustration. Suppose I draw a bee: it may not represent any particular kind of bee, but that does not mean that it is a drawing of something called a general bee. What is general is a concept, not an image.[4] I can think of plants or insects generally without thinking of particular plants or insects. As the mind can think of things generally, which is in another way than they exist in their matter, the mind is not material like them but immaterial.

> From the fact that the human mind knows the general natures of things, they (philosophers) perceived that the likeness by which we think of them is immaterial, otherwise it would be individuated and thus would not lead to general knowledge. But from the fact that the intelligible likeness is immaterial they perceived that the intellect is something that does not depend on matter.[5]

By an 'intelligible likeness' Aquinas means an idea or concept. If the mind were material, it could only think of things in the way that the senses know them, which is as individual things with their particular features. A horse always has hair of a particular colour but I can have the idea of a horse without thinking of a horse of a particular colour. One could object that this is not enough to show that the mind is immaterial, because gold is not in the eye materially when I look at some gold, but we do not say that sight is immaterial. Nonetheless, the impression of gold exists in the eye in the same way as gold exists in itself, which is in some matter. We do not just have impressions and images of horses and gold, for example, but also general ideas of these things.

Hume denied that we have general ideas. He thought that we only have ideas of particular things, which we call general by giving them a name that we apply to a greater number of similar things. 'All general ideas are nothing but particular ones annexed to a certain term which gives them a more extensive signification, and makes them recall upon occasion other individuals which are similar to them'.[6] This was because all ideas were copies of impressions for Hume, and impressions are of individual things. Thus Hume confuses concepts with mental images and more or less confines the mind to the imagination. It is, however, possible for us to think of abstract maxims without any images. For instance, I can think 'Brevity is the soul of wit' without any images coming into my mind. The mind cannot be material if I can have the concepts of immaterial things like brevity and wit. It is part of the concept of human beings that they have an understanding and reason, but understanding and reason are not material differences of human nature.

Numbers

Human beings are also distinguished from animals by the ability to count: animals cannot count things. This is because counting things involves having concepts. We count things under a concept: for example, seven stars, five continents, three hens, two governments. This itself requires having the concept of 'same'. We count things either as they are the same kind of thing or the number of different kinds of thing: there are fifty-seven ducks on the lake or their are seventeen different kinds of duck on the lake. 'How many animals are there in this zoo?'

may mean how many individual animals altogether or how many different kinds of animal.

Numbers are either things that exist in themselves or they are things of the mind. Either way they are immaterial objects. The German mathematician and philosopher, Gottlob Frege (1848-1925), argued that, as numbers are neither the properties of things nor subjective ideas, they must be objects of some kind. Ten is not the property of any one of the ten moons of Jupiter, for instance. We do not get the concept of number by abstracting it from objects. Nor are numbers subjective ideas, for we do not each have our own idea of ten or four. So Frege though that they are objects; only they are not actual (*wirklich*) objects, because numbers cannot do anything. He also thought it significant that we talk about, for example, 'the number four', as though it were an object.[7]

The Cambridge mathematician, G. H. Hardy (d.1947), regarded numbers as being as real as the objects we touch and see. Besides the physical reality that scientists study, there also exists a 'mathematical reality'.[8] Some think that mathematical reality is 'mental' because we construct mathematics ourselves, but others think that it exists outside of us and independently. We cannot alter the properties of numbers or make them do what we want. Scientists may argue whether we see things as they really are, but there is no disagreement about the properties of numbers: these are quite definite. The number six, for example, has the property of being the sum of the whole numbers by which it is divisible. The number 317 has the property of being a prime number and the sum of two integral squares ($11^2 + 14^2$). Thus Hardy claims that mathematicians get closer to reality than scientists, because the objects they deal with are quite definite. The properties of geometrical figures, like circles and triangles, remain unaltered even when the drawings used to illustrate them are inexact. Whether numbers are real objects, as Hardy thought, or are 'beings' of the mind, they are immaterial. But grasping immaterial objects is not the power of anything material.

Even a materialist like van Quine readily admits that abstract objects exist. 'Abstract objects have long since proved indispensable to natural science - thus numbers, functions and classes.'[9] Natural science cannot do without immaterial things like laws, constants and inverse square. Quine himself uses the abstract word 'entity' a great deal more frequently than a materialist should allow himself. He also says that we should not use abstract terms like peace, resolution or frankness unless one admits abstract objects. But abstract objects do no exist on their own, as Plato thought: they exist in minds. It is hard to explain how we come to have abstract objects unless the mind itself is immaterial.

Understanding

All material activities are processes, but understanding is not a process. Understanding may come as the result of a process of thinking and reasoning but is itself more like intuition. Mathematicians, for example, sometimes see the solution of a problem before they see the steps that lead to it. Poincaré once suddenly saw the solution of a problem he had been thinking about earlier as he crossed the road, even though he was not thinking about it at the time. When he reached home, he took one hour to write out the answer of what he had seen in a moment. Understanding is not the working out of a question but seeing or grasping something. It is not doing something in the mind but recognizing the principle with which to do it. For example, understanding enables me to continue this series of numbers: 1, 5, 11, 19, 29 when I see that the law of their sequence is $n^2 + n-1$. (If $n = 3$, $3^2 + 3 - 1 = 11$; if $n = 4$, $4^2 + 4 - 1 = 19$, and so on. So the next number after 29 will be 41.)

Although one may talk about 'processes' of reasoning, because we think in steps when we reason, I want to maintain that thinking is not material like sensation. Sensation occurs in a continuous stream, but even when we have a continuous series of thoughts, the thoughts are distinct. Thoughts often occur discontinuously: that is, we cannot reckon the interval of time between one thought and the next. Thus thinking is not a material activity. It is possible to identify our sensations with physical reactions in the nervous system and brain, but we cannot measure our thoughts like this on the scale of time.

I may think about something for a half-hour, but I could not say exactly when individual thoughts occurred within that half-hour. This difference between sensation and the mind is brought out by the way we say 'He was in pain all day' but not 'He understood all day'. Although we quite naturally say, 'A thought passed through my mind' or 'came into my mind', we do not say 'A thought passed through my brain'. Wittgenstein observes that when we say, 'I did not know what was going on in his head' we do not ordinarily mean brain-processes but thought-processes.[10]

If thinking is the power of any part of the body, it is of the brain. The brain seems to be what we think with, because we get tired in the head after a long time of hard thinking. The brain gets tired, however, because we cannot think without turning to images and using signs, which involve the brain. For example, we need to look at written signs and symbols to solve a problem of algebra. As G. H. Hardy observes, we use a chessboard or diagram to see a problem of chess more clearly, but the problem itself is abstract. This does not mean, however, that thinking itself is a power of the brain, only that the brain is involved in the exercise of thinking, because we need to turn to images and sense-data when we think about things. The brain provides the data *on which* we think. Peter Geach points out that the brain is not the organ of thinking as the eye is of seeing, because thinking is what he calls a 'basic activity', that is, an activity which we do not do by doing something else. I keep a diary by writing. I write sentences with a pen but I do not produce the thoughts contained in the sentences with the pen, for a sentence comes from thought.[11] Likewise, the vocal cords produce the sounds of words but they do not put together words in their grammatical order; grammar does not come from a material organ but from thought. For one thing, grammar is logical. The source of much of our activity is thought. Thinking is done *with* the brain, because we need images, but not *by* the brain. We do not think unless we have a mind, but the mind is not a part of the body as the brain is. As thought is the source of much of our activity, the mind is something that *moves itself*. We do not

just think when we are moved by something else but can have
spontaneous thoughts and sudden insights.

Self-Reflection

In order to do many things, we need to reflect on what we are
doing. David Braine observes that we do not use words without
reflecting on the words we put together. When I form a sentence,
I also know whether it is true or false.[12] Computers do not know
whether the information they give is true or false; they just give
the information. A computer no more knows anything than
a book does. Roger Penrose notes that computers work with
algorithms. An algorithm is a procedure for doing something:
for example, Euclid devised an algorithm for obtaining the
highest number by which any two numbers are divisible, say
27 and 15. But selecting the right algorithm for the work one
wants to be done is not itself an algorithmic process. We do
not decide which algorithm to use with another algorithm but
with judgement or insight.[13] Knowing the truth is itself a kind
of self-reflection, because it is not just knowing true things but
knowing that what one knows is true.

I have already given reasons why nothing material can
reflect on itself in Chapter Two. The things that reflect are
mirrors. It is possible for a mirror to reflect itself, by reflecting a
mirror opposite to it which reflects it. Mirror A reflects mirror
B, but as mirror B also reflects mirror A, the reflection of mirror
B in mirror A also contains mirror B's reflection of mirror A.
Thus a reflection of mirror A is seen in itself. But this is not
reflecting *on* itself, which is what the mind can do. A mirror can
only reflect itself by means of another mirror, but self-reflection
is an intrinsic activity: it is not done by anything external. St
Augustine remarks that when the mind thinks of itself, the
mind is in itself.[14] Nothing material can be in itself: I can put a
smaller box inside a larger one, but a box or sphere cannot get
inside itself. When something exists in itself by its own activity,
as the mind is in itself when it thinks of itself and its activity, it
is something subsistent. The mind's activities include judging,
deciding, willing, comparing, hoping, imagining, reasoning
and so on. Aquinas remarks that only the powers of knowing

which are powers of a bodily organ do not know themselves.[15] The eye sees outside objects but it does not know itself, because it does not see or know that it sees. The power of sight does not subsist in itself, because it does not know its own knowing; but it subsists in some matter. But the mind is *immediately* in itself when it reflects on itself, whereas a mirror only reflects itself indirectly through something outside itself.

Thus the mind is not only immaterial but also something subsistent, or rather the power of something subsistent, since it has activities and powers which are not the powers of anything material, such as having concepts, understanding and self-reflection. It is reasonable to suppose that, as sight and hearing are powers of something, namely of the organs of the eye and ear respectively, so thinking and understanding are the powers of something, but not of any bodily part. As they are not powers of body, they must be of something else - the soul. If the human soul has powers of its own that do not depend on the body, it is something that can exist on its own, as it has activities of its own. But how can one say that the soul is subsistent without falling back into dualism, because this seems to imply that a human being consists of two substances: a body and a subsistent soul? We shall deal with this question in the next chapter.

NOTES

[1] *A Treatise of Human Nature* I Appendix (1740).

[2] *Ibid.* I iii 14 (Selby-Bigge 157)

[3] *Nicomachean Ethics* II c.1, 1103a 30.

[4] *Has Mankind One Soul?* (The Casassa Lecture, Milwaukee 1985) 11.

[5] Aquinas, *De Veritate* 10,8.

[6] *Treatise of Human Nature* I i 7 (Selby-Bigge 17).

[7] *The Foundation of Arithmetic* (1884 Blackwell 1978) 57.

[8] *A Mathematician's Apology* (1940 Cambridge 1992) 123.

[9] *The Pursuit of Truth* (Cambridge, Mass. 1992) 25.

[10] *Philosophical Investigations* I 427.

[11]   What Do We Think With? in *God and the Soul* (Routledge & Kegan Paul 1979) 33.

[12]   *The Human Person* (Duckworth 1993) 380.

[13]   *The Emperor's New Mind* 536.

[14]   *De Trinitate* X 8, 11.

[15]   *Summa Theologiae* 1a 14, 2 ad1.

6

BODY AND SOUL

To many people it seems that, if the mind is immaterial and hence not a power of the body, we cannot avoid dualism. There are two ways of keeping the immateriality of the mind but avoiding dualism. One is simple to leave out the soul, as Sir Anthony Kenny does. The other is to make the mind a power of the soul that is the form of the body, which is the solution of St. Thomas Aquinas. In this chapter, I want to set out these two views and show why we do not need to omit the soul in order to avoid dualism.

A Capacity for Capacities

Anthony Kenny defines the mind as 'a capacity for capacities'. Here he returns to the tradition of Aristotle, who called the mind a power (*dunamis*). But where Aristotle makes the mind a power of the soul, Kenny leaves out the soul. The mind is a capacity for capacities, Kenny says, because all human beings have by nature the capacity to learn a language and to acquire some intellectual abilities. This capacity is realized by learning particular languages and other intellectual abilities, such as reading music or doing algebra. Intellectual abilities are activities which involve operating with symbols: 'the mind is a capacity to operate with symbols'.[1] These symbols are, in the first place, the signs of language, because it is by means of words that we explain other signs and symbols, such as those of mathematics and musical notation. Every human being has the capacity to learn a language, and this capacity is realized by having the capacity to speak a particular language, say, Hungarian or Chinese. Knowing a language is a capacity, because the capacity remains in me even when I am not speaking or thinking in that language or am asleep, for I can exercise the capacity at any time that I want. Learning a language is the primary capacity of human beings, because we learn everything else by means of words: how to tell the time, to distinguish colours or to work a computer.

Capacities, however, do not just exist on their own: a capacity is always the capacity of something. One could say that knowing a language and other intellectual abilities are capacities of the mind, but this answer is insufficient because Kenny has defined the mind itself as a capacity: it is 'a capacity for capacities'. This leaves us asking, What is the mind a capacity of? Kenny answers: 'My intellect and my will are in essence capacities. What are they capacities of? Of the living human being, the body you would see if you were here in the room where I write'.[2] For Kenny, what I am is a body: I have arms, legs, toes and so on. I also have a mind. But I do not have a body, Kenny says: I *am* a body. This means that the mind must be a capacity of the body. But this will not do for several reasons. For one thing, the mind is not a capacity of the body in the same way as sight is of the eye, for the mind *transcends* the body in the way it can think of things apart from their matter in an immaterial way, as Kenny himself acknowledges. When I see a cat I see it with a particular colour, but I can think of the shape of a cat without thinking of the colour of its fur.[3]

This answer, that the mind is a capacity of the body, is also contradicted by Kenny himself, since a little later he writes: 'in the present life there are intellectual and volitional activities which do not involve any bodily activity, such as silent thought'.[4] If I am a body and the mind is a capacity of this body, as Kenny says it is, it is not clear how I could have an activity, such as silent thought, which does not involve the body, I cannot just be a body if I can think silently. We have then to show how we can predicate silent thinking of someone, although the mind is not a capacity of the body. This can only be done if I am more than just a body and the mind is the capacity of something that is related to the whole of me.

It is only by a slight of hand, so to speak, that Kenny can say: 'though thinking is not the operation of any bodily organ, it is the activity of a body, namely the thinking human being'.[5] If thinking is not the operation of any bodily organ, it cannot be the activity of a body. I agree with Kenny that, although thinking is not the operation of any bodily organ, it is the activity of a human being. But I disagree with him that it is the activity of a body. How then can I show that thinking is not the activity of a body but it is the activity of a human being and not just of a mind? For Descartes, it is a mind rather than a human being who thinks, because he says that what he is is a thinking substance or his soul. The soul for Descartes is just the mind. Thus Descartes isolates thinking from the body in a purely mental sphere. It seems to me, however, that by leaving out the soul Anthony Kenny falls into the very fault which it is his express intention to avoid. For if the mind is not a capacity of the body, as it cannot be if, on Kenny's admission, thinking is not the operation of any bodily organ, it is isolated unless it is the capacity of that by which the body lives and moves. This is the soul. Kenny does not consider what makes the body that he says he is alive. This cannot be the mind, because the mind is a capacity.

A Power of the Soul

It is here that St Thomas Aquinas' solution comes in. For St Thomas the mind, or intellect, is a power of the soul which is the form of the body. The mind is a power, because we are not always actively thinking. Thus a human being thinks, and not just a mind, although the mind is not the capacity of the body, because the soul is united to the body as its form. 'Therefore it can be said that the soul (*anima*) thinks, as the eye sees; but it is more correct to say that a human being thinks by means of the soul.'[6] And this is just what Kenny would want to say: that it is not just a mind but a human being that thinks. Only Aquinas shows how this is possible when the mind is not a capacity of the body, by making it a power of the soul. A human being thinks, and not just a mind, because the soul is united to the body *as a whole*.

There are, however, two major difficulties about Aquinas' view, which I shall now face. The first is: if the soul is defined by its rational powers, how can it be the form of the body when these are not powers of the body? Or, to put it another way: how is the soul united to the body as its form when thinking is not the activity of a part of the body? The second difficulty is: if the soul is subsistent because it is immaterial, as I concluded at the end of the last chapter, how can we show that a human being is not two things after all but one? In other words, how does Aquinas' position avoid dualism?

If the soul is defined by its rational powers, so that we can call the soul 'the mind' after its highest power, do we not equate the soul with the mind, as Descartes did? But we would not say that the mind is the form of a human being. For one thing, as we have noted above, the mind is a capacity, so not the actuality of the body. The soul, however, is not just the mind, because it also has other powers: of growth, movement and sensation. Its rational powers only define the soul because they are what make the human soul specifically different. The soul is not any one of its powers but, as Aquinas explains, the powers of the soul are rooted in its essence.[7] The soul is not identical with its powers, because the soul still has these powers even when they are not active. It is by being rooted in the essence of the soul that the various powers of the soul have a unity, so that all our living activities stem from one source. Many powers of the soul are of something joint, because they can only be exercised with a part of the body: nothing has sensation without a soul but there is no sensation without a body. The soul is the cause of the powers of a living body: it is alive, moves, perceives and thinks because of the soul. These powers flow from the soul. The soul is the subject of the powers, like thinking and understanding, which are not powers of a bodily part, but a human being thinks and not just his soul or mind, because the soul also has powers which are not powers of the soul alone but of the joint thing of body and soul together, as they cannot be exercised without the body. Although the mind is not a power of the body, it is

the power of the soul that is united to the body because of its
other powers, such as sensation and seeing, which are powers
of the joint thing of body and soul. Body and soul are united,
because the soul alone is not the subject of all its powers, but
something joint is the subject of the powers that cannot be
exercised without the body.[8] Thus the soul can be the form of
the body, although thinking is not the activity of any bodily
part, because it also has other powers which are powers of the
body. The mind is only the highest of its powers, which enables
us in some way to transcend the body in our way of knowing.
Although thinking is not a power of the body, we need the
body, however, for our way of thinking because we only think
of things generally by first turning to images of things which we
perceive with the senses of the body. For example, we turn to
figures to see a problem in chess more easily.

We now turn to the second difficulty: When people think
that, if the soul is subsistent, a human being must consist of two
substances, a body and a soul, they assume that the body is a
substance without asking themselves what makes the body be
a substance in the first place. We saw, in the third chapter, that
a body is only a substance of any kind as long as it is a living
substance. When it loses its principle of life, which is its form,
it ceases to be a substance belonging to any kind or species, and
disintegrates. Thus a body is only a substance because of what
makes it alive, which is the soul. The body is not a substance on
its own but through the soul. Even when the soul is a subsistent
thing, a human being is not two substances because there is
a *substantial union* of body and soul. Being subsistent does
not prevent the soul from being the form of the body because,
as Aquinas remarks, the human soul is not contained by the
body but rather *comprehends* it as it is raised above the body,
or transcends it, by its way of knowing. The soul anyway gives
the body its unity. Body and soul make one being, because they
share *a single existence*. The body only exists as a body in union
with its soul. Although the human soul is subsistent because it
has an activity which does not depend on the body, like self-
reflection, it does not have a separate existence from the body

as long as the body is alive. Rather the soul gives the body its existence.

This, however, raises a further problem. If I am not my soul, the soul is a part of a human being. But if the soul is a part, it is inherent. And if it is inherent, it cannot also be subsistent. Aquinas maintains that a human being is not his or her soul, because whatever is a human being is something that has the complete nature of a human being, which includes having a body. So the soul is a part of human nature. How can the human soul then also be subsistent? The solution of this dilemma runs along the lines of saying that the soul is subsistent, although it is a part of a human being, because it is not partly present in different parts of the body, but is wholly present in every part and in the whole body. It can be wholly present in every part and in the whole, because it is not material.

In this chapter, we have reviewed Kenny's theory of the mind, which keeps the immateriality of the mind with the unity of the human being by leaving out the soul. Kenny presents the opposite view to Descartes: for Descartes what I am is my soul, for Kenny I am a body and have a mind. But Kenny is unable satisfactorily to explain what the mind is a capacity of, since we have activities like silent thought, which do not involve the body. Here Aquinas' view is more complete: the mind is a capacity, or power, of the soul which is united to the body as its form. Although Aquinas regards the human soul as something subsistent, this does not lead him into dualism, because there is a substantial union of body and soul: the body is only a substance in union with its soul. When we discard the view that the soul is the form of the body, the alternatives are that either we keep the soul but lose sight of the unity of a human being, like Descartes, or preserve the unity but make the mind a capacity of the body.

The next question is: since the soul is immaterial, how does it come to be in a human being and when? A first step to answering this question will be to consider the origin of language. As the mind is a capacity for intellectual abilities, which we exercise by operating with the symbols and signs of words, it is now common to define human beings as *linguistic* rather than rational animals. Thus we should be able to explain the intellectual abilities of human beings by discovering the origin of language. If language can be explained by evolution, we can explain the mind by evolution too. But, as language presupposes the ability to think, for a string of words has no sense unless they come from thought, the question of the origin of language will lead us to the question of the origin of the soul. This will be the subject of our inquiry in the next two chapters.

NOTES

1   *The Metaphysics of Mind* (Oxford 1989) 46.
2   *Ibid.* 17.
3   *Ibid.* 134.
4   *Ibid.* 31.
5   *Aquinas on the Mind* (Routledge 1993) 124.
6   *Summa Theologiae* 1a 75, 2 ad3.
7   *Ibid.* 1a 77, 1.
8   *Ibid.* 1a 77, 5 ad 1.

7

THE ORIGIN OF LANGUAGE

In the previous chapter, we saw that Kenny defines the mind as a capacity for capacities. We do not get a mind by thinking, but a child thinks for the first time because it already has this capacity. Other writers, however, think that our minds are made by the external influence of the surrounding culture in which we grow up and live. The British philosopher, John McDowell, for example, supposes that human beings are born as animals and are transformed into thinkers by *Bildung*, that is, by education. *Bildung* occurs through learning a language. The soul, McDowell says, is second nature: that is, it does not belong to us from the start by nature but we acquire it. For McDowell, the soul is equivalent to reason: we do not have it before we begin to reason.[1]

Don Cupitt thinks that the mind is made out of language.[2] This seems a reasonable view, because we think with words. Plato called thinking 'a dialogue of the soul with itself'.[3] What makes this view plausible, as Cupitt remarks, is that a clear thinker is someone who speaks clearly. But we could equally well say that someone speaks clearly because he or she thinks clearly. As words only have a meaning because they express conceptions of thought, language presupposes thought. Thus someone is not a clear thinker because he speaks or writes clearly, but he speaks clearly because he thinks clearly. Although it is true that our capacity for thought is widened by learning new words and thus acquiring new concepts, initially language is the product of the mind, not the mind the product of language.

For a similar reason, our minds are not just the product of culture. Culture is built up from one age to the next by transmitting ideas through a material medium either of the written and printed word or of the plastic arts. But no one would have been influenced by the thoughts of Sophocles, or Archimedes, or Newton, unless these thinkers had first had their thoughts. These were *original* thinkers. No one's mind would be shaped by Newton's laws of motion unless he had had the insight to discover them. Some say that we are programmed by our cultural environment, and that this programme constitutes our identity. This cannot be quite true because, however much we owe to others for our ideas, we are free to choose which elements of the surrounding culture to absorb or to reject. Our minds are not merely the products of culture, because no one can be 'programmed' by culture unless he or she has the capacity to receive this programme. As we know, programmes first need to be made; a programme presupposes thought. Even though the stock of ideas in someone's mind may largely come from others, from our teachers and the writers we and they have read, the mind does not just consist of its ideas since it is an active power that can produce its own thoughts and can reason about what it knows. Thus the theory that the soul or mind is made by culture presupposes the very thing that it is meant to explain.

There is no culture without tradition to hand it on, and, as Michael Dummett points out, there is no tradition unless 'language is the vehicle of thought and the instrument of communication'. Thus, even if we accept the view that the mind is the product of culture, we have to go back to the origin of language in order to explain culture. But, as Dummett also notes, language is 'the vehicle of thought'. Our first step, then, is to find out whether language can be explained by evolution. If language cannot be explained by evolution, neither can the human mind, for language presupposes thought. There would be an unexplained gap.

Has Language Evolved?

In order to see whether language has evolved, we should first compare the linguistic ability of human beings with any such ability that animals may possess. Here we should note certain differences between the language of human beings and of animals. The two primary examples of animals with speech are parrots and chimpanzees. Parrots only imitate the sounds of words; they do not know what they mean. A parrot cannot *name* anything like the cage it is in, but children quickly learn to name objects. Nor can a parrot use the words it has acquired to form new sentences and express its own thoughts. This ability of human beings to make new sentences out of the words they have learnt is called 'generative grammar'. When someone just repeats words without understanding them, we say that he talks like a parrot. Using words to express our own thoughts involves understanding. Chimpanzees have been taught to acquire a repertoire of words, but once children have passed the initial stages of learning language (first using phrases of one word and then of two or three words), they rapidly outstrip chimpanzees in their capacity for learning and communicating. A major difference between humans and other animals is that animals do not ask questions, but a child can already ask many questions by the age of three. This comparison of human beings with parrots and chimpanzees suggests that human language has not evolved from some rudimentary language of animals. The difference in linguistic ability between human beings and even chimpanzees, who are the nearest animal to us in the scale of evolution, shows that it is not just part of a gradual transition. Sir John Lyons, a professor of linguistics, has said that not only are we unable to show that human language has evolved from animal language but there is not even any evidence that any one of the thousand or so languages we know has evolved from simple ones.[4]

Whatever language animals and birds possess, it is very limited compared with the vastly more developed possibilities of human languages. It consists mainly of calling one to another and giving warning signs. The sounds that animals make have no grammar or syntax. We are told that whales hold long conversations under-water, but these probably consist of returning pleasing sounds to one another. We have no need to suppose that they tell stories or discuss things. These activities involve reflecting on what we do as well as having the conception of one thing coming after another, but animals have no conception of time. We can be fairly certain that whales do not put words or sounds together with syntax.

Those who think that human language is explained by evolution usually say that language developed with the evolution of the human brain. Karl Popper even thought that language has influenced the evolution of the human brain. He thought that language was the first product of the human mind and that 'the human brain and the human mind evolved in interaction with language'.[5] Although we can speak of an evolution of language and an evolution of thought, as one influences the other, language is not explained by the evolution of the brain, because the evolution of the brain was complete before the appearance of human language. Interestingly, the language areas of the brain are not found in the brains even of our closest ancestors, the apes. There is no Broca's area in other anthropoids: 'No area corresponding to the anterior speech area of Broca has been recognized in apes'.[6] Broca's area concerns speech production and fluency. Wernicke's area in the centre of the left hemisphere of the brain is the one for the interpretation of signs and semantic ability. Broca's area is the only new area of the cerebral cortex to have appeared in the evolution of the human brain.

As the language areas of the brain do not represent a stage in the evolution of language from animals, human language is not explained by evolution. The present state of the question, John Lyons says, is that linguists do not think the question can be decided one way or the other. Thus, for the time being, we are not going to be able to show that language is the result of evolution. In Lyon's view, we can say that human beings are physiologically disposed to voice sounds and communicate by means of the sounds they produce, because the vocal apparatus is more developed and in a better position than in chimpanzees. But 'What it (the evidence) does not prove - though it is often so interpreted - is that they (humans) are genetically programmed to learn spoken languages as such'.[7] The development of the instrument of speech does not by itself explain the ability to use language, because neither the brain nor vocal cords arrange words in their grammatical order. Sentences come rather from thought.

Universal Grammar

The best known version of the idea that we are genetically programmed to learn language is Noam Chomsky's theory of universal grammar. Noticing that the similarities between languages are greater than their differences, Chomsky proposed that this is explained by something called 'universal grammar'. We see that languages have a similar structure, because we can translate one language into another. According to Chomsky, the grammatical structure of all languages is determined by a specific set of principles. These principles include the notions of number (singular and plural), tense and negating sentences. Universal grammar also includes the categories of quality, relation and action, of classifying things according to kinds, and the rule for transforming statements into questions by reversing the position of the subject word and verb. Chomsky also holds that universal grammar is innate, since every child is born with the disposition for recognizing its principles.

Although Chomsky's theory of universal grammar seemed to be a return to innate ideas when it was first announced, Chomsky developed it in order to *combat* the theory of innate ideas. For Chomsky does not think that we possess ideas innately that have come to us from outside, either from self-existing ideas, like Plato, or from God, like Descartes. As he does not believe that innate ideas have been put into us from outside, he has to show that the principles of generative grammar come to be in us innately by another route. Since he does not think that we have souls, he is compelled to explain universal grammar by some material means. His theory is that universal grammar is innate because it is genetically determined. According to Chomsky, universal grammar is genetically innate like the instructions in the genes for growing arms and legs.[8] Although the ability to learn language is innate in the sense that it belongs to human nature, that does not necessarily mean that it is part of our biological nature. For the principles that govern language are *logical* rather than biological.

A few examples will suffice to show this. First, to use one of Chomsky's own examples, the difference between 'Everyone betrayed the woman he loved' and 'The woman he loved betrayed everyone' rests on logic. By converting the position of subject and object in the first sentence, we alter the universality of the verb from everyone betrays someone (each a different person) to someone betrays everyone. Universal grammar would not produce logical results like this if it was produced genetically. Even if universal grammar were genetically determined, nature must have known how to write the programme for it, unless it was constructed at random. It cannot have been random, because grammar is logical. Language cannot be both genetically determined *and* logical unless the source of nature that is genetically determined is itself some mind. Language and syntax cannot arise from nature by itself, because nature obeys the laws of physics but languages include many exceptions to the rule (for which there is usually a reason) and irregularities. It is no accident, for example, that the verbs we use most often, like to be, to have, to see, to come, to go and to drink, are irregular. These irregularities are due to human decision and custom, and are sometimes for the sake of a pleasing variation of sound.

Quite apart from whether or not it is genetically determined, universal grammar does not by itself explain the mind, because it is no more able to generate language or thought than the rules of chess are able to generate a game of chess. As the rules of chess are not genetically determined but were invented by one or more minds, it seems that, if universal grammar exists and is innate in us, its source too is a mind: either our mind or some greater mind.

Not everyone agrees with Chomsky that universal grammar is the reason why children are able to recognize the principles of language. Lyons notes that a child does not have a mental language before it acquires a particular language, but it learns grammar by learning a particular language, its native language. This rules out Chomsky's idea that universal grammar is innate, since grammar is acquired rather than innate.[9] Although

Chomsky maintains that universal grammar exists, writers about linguistics do not rule out the possibility that languages have a similar structure because they have a common origin.

Two further arguments stand in the way of Chomsky's theory of universal grammar. First, if language has not evolved, as it cannot be shown to have done, the principles of its grammar cannot be genetically determined, as Chomsky says they are. Secondly, as language that has rules cannot have evolved by chance, universal grammar is again not explained by genetics. This second point is taken up by Kenny when he argues that evolution does not explain human language, because it is *conventional*.

No Natural Origin

Kenny points out that human language is not the result of evolution, because it is not natural but conventional. Language is conventional, because it is governed by rules and human beings have agreed which sounds mean what. The meaning of words is established by convention. Language is natural in the sense that the capacity to use it is part of human nature, but it does not come from nature because its rules have not evolved by nature, for they are logical. Language with rules has not come about through evolution because, as Kenny remarks, it is contrary to the very idea of rules that they are hit upon by chance as, say, the discovery of raising dough with yeast or fermenting with alcohol may have been made by chance. Doing things with rules has not evolved from animals, because they do not have rules for doing things, as we have for all sorts of areas of social life: exchanging contracts, electing governors, inheriting property, passing one another on the road or at sea.

The signs of language are also conventional, because they have been *invented*. In order to invent something, the inventor first needs to conceive the purpose of his invention. When the invention is language, one already needs language, Kenny says, in order to conceive its purpose.[10] Thus language is what he calls *intentional*: we know what it is and what it is for. You cannot possess a language and not know what it is, because one of the words of a language is a word for 'word' (*logos, verbum, mot, palabra, parola, Wort* and so on). To use the word 'word', or its equivalent, is to know what a word is and what it is for. Animals know neither of these things.

Kenny also notes that, if language came about through evolution, it was by a mutation in an individual. But language cannot have first occurred like this, Kenny says, because using a language presupposes a community of people, both for learning a language and to have someone to communicate one's thoughts to. Kenny, however, leaves unanswered the question of how the first users of language arose: it must have appeared all at once, since its members did not have anyone from whom they could learn language. Although speaking a language involves a community with which to share one's thoughts, it is possible that language first appeared with an individual, because language presupposes *thinking,* as it is for communicating one's thoughts. It is no more difficult, however, to suppose that language first appeared in an individual, or the first pair of human beings, than that a whole community of language users suddenly appeared when there had been no language before them. Although Kenny requires a community for the appearance of language, elsewhere he says that the best account of the origin of language is to be found in the book of *Genesis,* chapter one.[11] This tells us that language first existed in one human being, or one pair, who gave names to all the different natural kinds of beast (and presumably plants).

If, as Kenny notes, we cannot invent language without first conceiving its purpose, but in order to conceive its purpose we already need to possess language, his own argument leads us to think that language does not have a merely human origin but our capacity to use language comes from some higher source.

When Kenny points out that language requires a community, he reminds us of one of the lessons to be learnt from Wittgenstein (1889-1951), who teaches us that language presupposes a community, because there is no such thing as a private language. (A private language is one that just I use for myself, in which I give words my own meanings.) But for the beginning of language, Wittgenstein supposed that it must have been different.

On the other hand, language has certainly come about naturally, i.e., there must presumably have been a first man who for the first time expressed a definite thought in spoken words. And besides the whole question is a matter of indifference because a child learning a language only learns it by beginning to think in it. Suddenly beginning; I mean there is no preliminary stage in which a child already has a language, so to speak uses it for communicating but does not yet think in it.[12]

Here Wittgenstein clearly holds that language presupposes thinking, because no one can use language for communicating without being able to think in it. But a child suddenly thinks for the first time. If this is true of any child, it was also true of the first human being. There were no stages in evolution towards thinking: one either has a thought or not. We learn a language but we do not teach a child to think; it just does it.

In this chapter, we have seen that human language is not explained by evolution for two reasons. First, there is no gradual transition from an animal language to human language. Secondly, language presupposes the capacity to think, but this is not the power of a bodily organ. Thus the question of the origin of language has led us to that of the origin of our power to think. How did this power come to be in the first human being when it did not evolve? And how does this power come to be present in each subsequent human being: is it passed on by generation or does it come to be in each human being in some other way? These are questions that I shall deal with in the next chapter.

NOTES

[1] *Mind and World* (Harvard 1994) 125.

[2] *Creation out of Nothing* (London, SCM 1990) 157-159.

3   *Sophist* 263e. *Theaetetus* 189e: 'Thinking is the speech (*logos*) which the soul runs through with itself'.

4   *Semantics* (Cambridge 1977) 85.

5   *The Self and its Brain* (Routledge 1977) 11.

6   J.C. Eccles, *Evolution of the Brain* (Routledge 1989) 89.

7   *Natural Language and Universal Grammar* (Cambridge 1991) Vol I 88.

8   *Rules and Representations* (Blackwell Oxford 1980) 91.

9   *Semantics* 82.

10   *The Development of Mind*, with H.C. Longuet, J.R. Lucas & G.H. Waddington (Edinburgh 1973) 95.

11   *Ibid.* 91.

12   *Philosophical Remarks* (1930 Blackwell 1975) no. 5.

8

THE ORIGIN OF THE SOUL

When Aristotle reflected on the question about where the power of thinking comes from, he discerned that the mind (*nous*) is not the power of the seed, as he put it, but 'comes in from outside'. This was because Aristotle thought that the mind, or intellect, is immaterial, and so could not be a power transmitted with matter. In Aristotle's view, the mind is, to begin with, potential for thinking of all kinds of things. This potential is actualized when the mind actively thinks of something. Aristotle did not think that it was possible for the mind to think of the natures of all kinds of material things if it shared material nature with any of them. In the same way, if we look at things through tinted glass we will not see them with their true colour but their colour will be affected by the colour of the glass through which we look at them. So Aristotle thought that the mind must be immaterial and not the power of any organ of the body. He notes that the mind differs from the senses, which have bodily organs, in that the organs of sense can be damaged by something exceptionally strong (very bright light or deafeningly loud sounds), whereas the mind is not affected in this way by its object when it thinks of something extremely clear.[1] The mind is also immaterial for Aristotle because it is a power, or capacity, for being things without their matter. This means, it can think of things in an immaterial way, not as they exist individually in matter, but generally, as was explained in Chapter Five, in the second section on concepts. As the intellect is immaterial, Aristotle did not think that it could be drawn from the seed (or chromosomes, as we should say today) but comes from elsewhere, perhaps from some higher mind or intellect.[2]

We may come to a conclusion similar to Aristotle's by thinking about an ordinary occurrence in everyday life. I return to my room and find fixed to the door a piece of paper with signs on it. As I understand these signs when I read them, they are *intelligible* signs. As they are intelligible signs they come from someone with intelligence. We recognize that certain signs are intelligible, because when we see the words of a language we know we often cannot help reading and understanding them, for example, the posters we pass in the street. If I can understand signs, so can the person who wrote them. Where did this person get the signs from? From someone else who learnt them from another person before him or her, and so on going all the way back to the inventor of the signs.[3] But unless the inventor of the signs was also the author of his intelligence, we have not explained the origin of human language, without going back to the source of intelligence in human beings. This must be some intelligent being. Since understanding is not the power of anything material, it seems that mind could only come from a Mind.

As intelligence has not risen from matter by itself, there are two possibilities. Either our mind is part of another, universal mind or the soul, of which the mind is a power, is created by God out of nothing, because it is immaterial. To create, in the proper sense, means to make out of nothing. An immaterial thing is not made out of anything. The first of these alternatives will be mentioned again with more detail in Chapter Ten. The second alternative is that my mind does not belong to another mind but, as it does not come from matter, it comes from outside because it is a power of the soul that has been brought into being by a direct act of creation. Not everyone today, however, understands the word 'create' in the traditional sense of to make out of nothing.

A Provision in Matter

Richard Swinburne, for example, says that souls are created, because they are immaterial. The soul is immaterial for Swinburne, because it has a mental life which cannot be explained by physics and chemistry.[4] Mental life cannot be explained by science, he says, because there are no laws for correlating sensations and thoughts with events in the brain. As the soul is immaterial it is created, but when Swinburne says that the soul is created he does not mean that it is created directly by God. For Swinburne the creation of the soul means that God made a provision that beings with a mental life which cannot be explained scientifically would arise from a certain part of his creation. This idea is found in John Locke (1632-1704), who thought it quite possible that God gave some systems of matter the power to perceive and think, without any need for us to suppose that this is the capacity of an immaterial substance added to the body, for it can come from matter that is suitably disposed. Locke also thought that matter was not even able to produce motion by itself. If all there was in the beginning was matter, he says, not even a pebble would have moved.[5] As matter is unable to move itself, how much less is it able to give rise to perception and mind of itself.

In Swinburne's estimation, when we say that something has a soul we mean that it has a mental besides a bodily life. To have a mental life is to know and experience things which are private to the subject who has them: sensations, images, thoughts, beliefs, desires etc. As animals also have a mental life, according to Swinburne, because they too have sensation but sensation is a different event from the brain-event that causes it, for an image is not itself physical, he says that animals also have souls and these animal souls too are created.[6] This surely leaves too little distinction between animal and human souls when we have already noted some vast gaps between animals and human beings in their powers of thinking with concepts and understanding, not to mention self-reflection. To say that animals have a mental life, in a curious way, has resulted from Descartes who denied that animals were conscious, because they are not conscious that they exist. As whatever we are conscious of are thoughts, thus sensations and images are 'thoughts' for Descartes, and thoughts belong to a thinking substance, so sensations became mental with him. But once you recognize, as Descartes did not, that animals too have sensation and are conscious, it was a short step to saying that they too have a mental life. A further consequence has been that, as sensation is material because it depends on bodily organs, but it is now counted as mental, so it became natural to say that the mind too is material, just as sensation is. This, however, is the exact opposite of what Descartes intended, for he asserted a clear distinction between mind and matter, thinking and extended substances.

Although Swinburne thinks that animal souls are immaterial, because they have a mental life, they are not immaterial in the sense of having an activity like thinking, which is not the power of a bodily organ. All their activities are limited to the senses and imagination, which require bodily organs (we only have images of things we have perceived through the senses). Thus the souls of animals do not survive, because they have no power which is not the power of a bodily part. We have already noted that for the ancient Greeks sensation was quite distinct from reason (*logos*); they would never have called sensation 'mental': only thought and reason belonged to the mind (*nous*), as distinct from the soul, the principle of life. Swinburne too easily regards animal souls as immaterial like human souls, without arguing sufficiently for their immateriality. Aquinas drew a much sharper division between the material and immaterial and restricted the immaterial to the intellect and will, because only these are not a power or function of the body. Imagination falls on the material side for Aquinas, since images come through the senses, which are material. The will is immaterial, because free will goes with reason and seeing alternative courses of action. Animals have some kind of choice, but their choice is limited to what is present to their senses. They do not conceive rational ends, such as foregoing pleasure for some higher end or goal. The will is known as the *rational* appetite as distinct from the appetites of our sensitive nature.

Swinburne combines two positions, which most people think exclude one another. On the one hand, he says that the soul is created, because it is immaterial. On the other hand, he thinks it has evolved, which usually means from matter. But these two positions are not incompatible for Swinburne's view of creation, since the creation of the soul means for him that the Creator arranged that mental life would arise from some matter. One difficulty with this view is that the power must have already have existed in the matter, from which human beings evolved. If it already existed in the matter that formed the animals from which human beings evolved, why were not some of those animals also intelligent? One difference, however, between Swinburne and those who hold a materialist theory of evolution is that Swinburne thinks the Creator put this power into matter: it did not come from matter by itself or by chance.

Another version of the view held by Swinburne, that the soul is created but each soul is not created directly by God, was put forward by the catholic Jesuit theologian, Karl Rahner. According to Rahner, the creation of the soul means that God created the human species, because man is not just a modification of the tree of evolution, since a 'radical boundary' exists between human beings and the rest of nature. There is a radical boundary, because human beings are distinguished by self-consciousness and spirit. Rahner does not think that human beings have evolved, but he denies that each person's soul is specially created by God. To Rahner the special creation of the soul seemed like a miraculous intervention, which he says would be an unnecessary repetition after the creation of human species. Rahner assumes that human souls have a natural cause. So it seemed to him that, if God does what the parents can do, his making the soul directly would be a miracle within the order of nature, but miracles properly belong to the economy of salvation. According to Rahner, human beings are transcendent, because our knowledge tends towards the general, and two people transcend themselves in generating a unique individual.[7] Rahner allows us to say that God creates the soul in the sense that human beings act with the power that God has given them, but he says that the parents produce the soul immediately. A directly transcendent cause was only needed for the genesis of the human race, not for the soul of every human individual. To work a miracle, however, is to produce a natural effect without its *natural* cause, for example the physical healing of a diseased body. But as human souls do not have a natural cause, for they are immaterial, their making by God is not a miracle, as Rahner supposes. Thus Rahner's objection that the creation of individual souls would be 'a miraculous intervention' does not apply here, because bringing something immaterial like a human soul into existence does not anyway have a natural cause. One may say that the creation of the soul is an intervention in that God infuses the soul into the body newly conceived, but it is not, strictly speaking, a miracle because no natural cause is passed by. Rahner's view of the creation of the soul seems very like traducianism, that the soul is passed on by the parents. Perhaps Aristotle saw more clearly that the mind could not be transmitted in this way, because it is not a power of the body, but 'comes in from outside'. If the human soul is immaterial because of its powers of mind, as I argued in Chapter Five, it cannot be transmitted by matter, as Swinburne and Rahner think possible.

Animation

The alternative is that the soul with the power of understanding is directly created by God for each human being, because it is immaterial. God creates souls individually as new human beings are brought into existence. Souls do not pre-exist their bodies, as Plato thought. Origen's opinion that souls pre-exist was condemned by the Church at the Second Council of Constantinople, in 543. One reason for rejecting the pre-existence of souls is that if our souls pre-exist, so did Christ's, because he is like us in his human nature in every way but sin. But if his soul existed on its own before its union to divine nature, it had a personal existence of its own. Christ would not then be one person, as orthodoxy holds, but two, for the Incarnation would have been a union of two persons. As our souls do not pre-exist, the question is: When is the rational soul first present in a human being, at conception or some later stage? This is the question of animation or ensoulment.

Aristotle thought that there are three alternatives when a human being is generated:

1) either he has no soul to begin with, or
2) he has a vegetative and then a sensitive soul, or
3) he has the powers of all three kinds of soul (vegetative, sensitive and rational) from the start.

He discounts the first possibility, because there is no animal without some soul that enlivens it. He also rejects the third possibility, because he thought there was an animal before a human being. This view requires that the same individual exists as two different *kinds* of creature: first as an animal, then a human being. Although a human being is a kind of animal, a rational animal, the human soul constitutes an altogether different kind of animal because it is immaterial.

According to Aristotle, the soul comes into existence with the individual animal, as it is the form of the body. There is no soul in the seed or ovum, because these are not individual beings before they are fused into a new being with its own life. Aristotle says that the vegetative and sensitive souls are potentially in the seed, since it is by a power in matter that a vegetative soul turns into a sensitive one when the matter has developed sufficiently for having sentience. Unlike the intellectual soul, these two kinds of soul do not come from outside, because growth and sensation are inseparable from organs of the body. Aristotle's own view was that one soul turns into another kind of soul as an embryo develops. Thus the sensitive soul is not present before the body is capable of sensation, which is not before the neural cord appears in the third week.

Aquinas followed Aristotle in thinking that there is an animal soul before a human one, but he did not think that one kind of soul can turn into another kind. So he says that one soul succeeds another: when the higher soul comes into existence, it replaces the lower one, which then goes out of existence. But the higher soul includes the vegetative and sensitive powers of the lower souls. As the soul is the form of the human being, Aquinas did not think that the human soul was infused until the matter of the embryo was sufficiently organized and disposed to receive it. This would be when it is recognizably human. Aquinas thought this was about 40 days after conception. Although Aquinas says that no animal soul is present until movement and sensation are manifest, Elizabeth Anscombe points out that he does not say that there is no rational soul before there is rational activity. It follows from this observation that, if the rational soul can be present before the child reasons, it could be present from conception, because there is no way of determining how long before active reasoning it is present. Aquinas' view contains the same difficulty as Aristotle's: it requires the substantial change of the same individual from one kind into another, from an animal into a human being. As one soul goes out of existence when it is replaced by another, in Aquinas' view, this can only occur in an instant. But the growth of an embryo shows no clearly defined stages of transition when this might happen. As there is no clear way of assigning a definite point in the embryo's development when we might say the human soul enters, we may be inclined to say that it is present from the beginning, that is, from conception.

One point in favour of this view is that we know a zygote *already is a new individual being*, since it is not just an extended part of its mother. Although it is linked to its mother, it has a distinct life, because it absorbs the nourishment it draws from its mother by its own power. This was something that St Thomas Aquinas knew, for he remarks that the vital operations of the embryo are not the mother's, since nourishment and growth cannot be done by an external agent.[8] They are intrinsic powers of the individual. By recognizing this, the geneticist Jerome Lejeune, who discovered the defect in the chromosomes that causes Downe's syndrome, came to his argument for immediate animation. He starts off by saying that a zygote, which comes into existence at conception, is a distinct individual, for a distinct life begins when the ovum is fertilized. As natural science confirms that it is a human life, and we know that this zygote is going to turn into a human being, why is it not already a human being? It seems that, as we cannot say when some matter that is going to be a human being first becomes human, not having been human up to that point, there is no point before which it has not been a human being. Although someone who thinks that the human soul is not infused until after 13 days (the time up to which a zygote can split into twins), may argue that a zygote is human but not yet a human being, because it does not yet have the human soul, Lejeune argues that a zygote is a being (*un être*) and we know that it is human, so why is it not a human being?

One can argue against Lejeune that a group of blood or bone cells are a being and that they are human, because taken from a human being, but we do not call them a human being; so neither is a zygote a human being at first. Lejeune replies that there is this difference between a group of blood cells and the group of cells that constitutes a zygote: a group of blood cells is not going to turn into a human being but a zygote is. A zygote is a whole, unified being, but a group of blood cells has no existence of its own. What makes a group of cells into a human being, Lejeune says, is the human soul. The point of Lejeune's argument that a zygote is not just human but already a human being, is made clearer by the French terms: a zygote is not just *un être humain* but *un homme*.[9] Thus the human soul enters at conception.

One argument against animation at conception is the case of monozygotic twins. Monozygotic twins are twins that come from the same fertilized ovum. If the soul of every human being is infused at conception, then two souls must be present in one zygote before it splits, or else only one of the twins will have its soul from the moment of conception and the other only from the time when the zygote splits. Also only one of the twins will be identical with the original zygote and the other split from it. This is the point of the title of Elizabeth Anscombe's paper, *Were You a Zygote?* in which she discusses this question. The objection against thinking that two souls can be present in the same zygote from conception is that this requires the same unit to have two substantial forms at the same time, since a soul does not divide into two souls as a zygote may split into two. It would also mean that either one zygote has a double existence or two human beings share the same existence until the zygote divides. The case of monozygotic twins is an argument against immediate animation because, if the souls of both twins cannot be present from conception, we cannot say that every human being receives his or her soul at conception. Elizabeth Anscombe later changed her mind about the question, as we shall now see.

At first, she thought that the possibility of monozygotic twins up to the 13th day was a decisive argument against immediate animation. In her first paper on the topic, *Were You a Zygote?* she sets out four possibilities.

1. A zygote that is going to twin already is two human beings.
2. The zygote is one human being and an extra one grows out of it.
3. The zygote is one human being that splits into two human beings, as an amoeba divides into two new amoebae.
4. A zygote is a whole substantial entity but not yet a human being.

She said about the first possibility that there is not sufficient evidence for it. About the third possibility, she said that a zygote does not divide like an amoeba because we know that there is an amoeba before it divides but we do not know that there is a human being before the zygote divides. When an amoeba divides into two new amoebae, neither is identical with the original amoeba, which goes out of existence. As it is unthinkable that a human being should go out of existence in this way, a zygote cannot be a human being from the start. This leaves us with the second and fourth possibilities. She does not accept the second possibility, that a zygote is a human being, because only one of the twins would be identical with the original zygote. So she settled, at first, for the fourth possibility, that a zygote is not yet a human being: 'We cannot say yet that we have here two distinct animals'.[10]

Anscombe later completely reversed her opinion and argued that, if a zygote is going to twin, it already is two human beings.[11] She reached this conclusion by considering the following new set of possibilities.

1. A zygote is initially one human being that is going to become two human beings.

2. When the zygote twins, the initial human being no longer exists, as an amoeba ceases to exist when it divides into two new ones.
3. One of the twins is identical with the original human being that the zygote is, and the other springs from it.
4. The single cell already is two human beings from the start before the zygote divides.

We notice that the fourth possibility of the first list (a zygote is a human substantial entity but not yet a human being), which Anscombe adopted as her initial position, does not appear in this new list, because in the meantime she has heard the argument of Lejeune. Anscombe rejects the first and second possibilities of the new list, because they both imply that the initial human being ceases to exist. As it is impossible to say which of the twins is identical with the initial human being, we say that neither is, and the initial one has, therefore, ceased to exist. She merely says about the third possibility, 'there is no reason at all to think that this is what happens'. This leaves the fourth possibility alone. Anscombe's revised opinion requires that two human beings occupy the same space at the same time, if a single cell already is two human beings. Her response to this difficulty is that a miracle is always possible in the case of monozygotic twins. It is not apparent, however, that this solution is any more satisfactory than thinking that God makes a special provision for the fairly rare occurrence of a zygote splitting into two, by creating a new soul for the new being that splits from it. This is the third possibility in her new list (second in the old list): one of the twins is identical with the zygote and a new human being comes into existence when the zygote divides. Another widely held objection against immediate animation is that a considerable number of zygotes fail to develop and, as this happens naturally, the Creator would not infuse souls into beings that are not going to become viable embryos. It should, however, be remarked that the number of zygotes or embryos that fail is often exaggerated: it is one tenth rather than one fifth or even one third.

Perhaps it is a question that we shall never be able to decide with certainty. Even if we cannot *know* that the human soul is infused at conception, this still does not permit us to destroy zygotes up to the time when we think that they become human beings, because we should give the benefit of the doubt to something that might be a human being. Nor should we take it into our own hands to terminate the existence of something that we know has all the potential to become a human being. The possibility of cloning raises new questions. Would God create souls for embryos that have not come into existence by the fusion of male and female gametes but been 'engineered', so to speak? We cannot know the answer to this question until a human being has been produced by the technique of cloning. We have not yet heard of this succeeding. A sheep can be cloned, because the vegetative and sensitive souls are passed on with matter, but the human soul is not a power of matter. What we can say is that one reason why a human being may never be produced by cloning is that God would not infuse a soul into anything produced by this technique, so that this product never would have the form of a human being.

Whether the human soul is infused at conception or some later time, if the soul does not come with the body it comes *to* it. And if it comes to the body, it is *something* that comes to body. Thus the soul that comes to the body from outside, so to speak, is something subsistent, for what is created by God is something. The human soul comes from outside in that it does not come from matter and is created by God. It is neither part of some separate, universal mind, since we each have our own minds, nor does the creation of the soul mean that God made a special provision for some matter to carry the power of mind, which is tantamount to saying that mind is passed on as a power of matter. The alternatives are that either the human soul is specially created or it is traduced.[12] As the soul is not passed on by generation, because the mind and understanding are not the power of a material part, it is created by God. Perhaps the reason why human beings are the unique persons that we recognize them to be, is that the soul is not transmitted by the parents but is brought into existence entirely anew. The next step is to consider what is a person. This will help us to see further that the soul is a part of human nature.

NOTES

1 *De Anima* III c.4, 429a 10-429b 8.

2 *De Generatione Animalium* II c.3, 736 b28.

3 I owe this argument to G.E.M. Anscombe, *Human Essences* (unpublished paper). I have varied her example of finding scratches on a rock.

4 *The Evolution of the Soul* (Oxford 1986) 190.

5 *An Essay Concerning Human Understanding* IV c. 3, 6; IV c.10, 10.

6 *Loc. Cit.* 199.

7 *Theological Investigations* vol. 1 293; *Hominisation* (Herder 1965) 81-84, 98-101.

8 *ST* 1a 118, 2 ad 2.

9 I am indebted to Prof. G.E.M. Anscombe for telling me about Lejeune's argument.

10 Were You a Zygote? *Philosophy and Practice*, ed. A. Phillips Griffiths (Cambridge 1985) 115.

11 *Is Killing Zygotes Murder?* (unpublished paper given at St Louis, U.S.A., 1992).

12 Traducianism (that the human soul is transmitted by the parents) has been consistently rejected by the Catholic Church: by Pope Anastasius II in 498, Benedict XII in 1341, and Leo XIII in 1887.

9

PERSONS

In his long short story *Dr Jekyll and Mr Hyde*, Robert Louis Stevenson describes the attempt of someone to escape the conflict between the good and evil sides of his nature by separating the one from the other, so that each can pursue its way unchecked by the other: the good side without being dragged down by the bad, the bad without being reproved by the good. Stevenson's story is based on his conviction that a human being is not really one but two things and the body is an 'immaterial tabernacle', 'a mere aura and effulgence of certain powers that made up my spirit'. By taking a transforming drug compounded of crystalline salt, phosphorous and ether that turns from bright red to dark purple and, finally, watery green as the crystals dissolve when boiled, the doctor finds that his personality changes as his body changes into the squat, contorted figure of Edward Hyde. From now on he leads a double life between two selves: one of genial respectability, the other of dark depravity. Gradually his worse self takes over his better self and, in the end, as he has to take the drug ever more frequently in order to return to being Dr Jekyll, the small frame of Edward Hyde lies curled up on the floor, covered in the clothes of the large doctor. Is Stevenson's story a case of the same man being alternately two persons?

The story raises several philosophical, as well as moral, questions. To what extent is personality determined by physical factors? Or does the body reflect the personality? Is the body essential to a person? Are persons purely mental or is the body part of what a person is? What is a person anyway? Even if I could become another person, would I want to? 'What is a person?' and 'Can a person be two persons?' are questions about the identity of persons. Although this question is much discussed in present day philosophy, it hardly concerned philosophers in the Middle Ages. For centuries the definition of person given by Boethius (480-524) remained the standard one: a person is 'an individual substance of rational nature.' In other words, the identity of person was thought to have something to do with substance. This view remained until it was questioned by John Locke in the 17th century. Locke's view of persons continues to exercise a powerful, though often unacknowledged, influence on contemporary thinking about persons. The question of the identity of persons is important for our purposes, because there are two sorts of identity: one is the identity of the same individual *across time*, from moment to moment; the other is the identity of the *nature* of an individual with other individuals. Once you want to allow the possibility that a person is not totally extinguished at death, this second question, of the nature of the human person, becomes important if the person survives in some way when his or her body has ceased to exist.

The Same Consciousness

Locke argued, against a long tradition of philosophy, that identity of persons has nothing to do with substance in the following way, by first considering the identity of bodies. He notes that, as the identity of body does not consist in its matter, for its matter does not remain the same, it must consist in something else, which he says is the same *life*. 'An oak tree continues to be the same tree as long as it partakes of the same life, though that life be communicated to ever new particles of matter. Likewise, the identity of a human being consists in nothing but a participation of the same continued life, by constantly fleeting particles of matter, in succession vitally united to the same organized body.'[1] From this Locke concludes that identity of substance does not include all sorts of identity; so being the same person need not have to do with being the same substance. Note that, at this point, Locke talks about the identity of a human being, not of a person, for he wants to distinguish the two. We should also add

that Locke has no right to get away from substance, because new particles of matter are not simply united to the same life, since something has to have the life.

Locke, however, proceeds to draw the conclusion that as an animal or human being remains the same animal or human being, although it changes its body several times in the course of its life, so a person could change his body but remain the same person. This conclusion is a fallacy, because, although the matter of our body is totally renewed every seven years, we never change our bodies. A living body remains the same individual substance, although its matter is completely renewed. All that happens is that parts of the same body are changed one by one as its material constituents are continually renewed, but one body is never replaced by an entirely new one. Locke saw that the same living body does not depend on the *material* identity of its parts, but he forgot about *numerical* identity. The body of an old person is numerically the same body as he or she had when a child, although all its matter has been changed several times over, because the body of the aged person is continuous with the body of that person when young. As Locke thinks that a person can change bodies and the same man be several persons, he makes identity of person into something incorporeal, because it has nothing to do with the body for him.

Locke's view was that identity of persons has to do with the same *consciousness*. Consciousness for Locke is the perception of what passes in a man's own mind.[2] A person stands for 'an intelligent being that has reason and reflection and can consider itself.'[3] As a person is someone who can consider himself as himself, Locke goes on from saying that identity of person consists in consciousness, because it is by consciousness that everyone is to himself what he calls a *self*, to say that a person is a self. '*Person*, as I take it, is the name for this *self*'.[4] This is the origin of the modern view that a person is a self. There is some plausibility in Locke's view, because it is by consciousness that I know that my actions are my own and thus that I am distinct from others.

Identity of person then goes from consisting in consciousness to consisting in memory, because Locke says that there is the same person as far back or as far forward as the same consciousness extends to actions in the past or future. So, if I am conscious of the actions of Nestor, I am the same person with Nestor, Locke says.[5] The idea that identity of person depends on memory may, however, be questioned in many ways.

Bishop Joseph Butler (1692-1752) observes that very often the reason why I remember doing something is that *I* did it.[6] If the reason why I remember doing something mostly is that I did it, memory presupposes consciousness of one's personal identity rather than constitutes it.[7] Butler points out that the identity of a person is not identity of consciousness but of a living being, because consciousness of being the same person is consciousness of being the same substance. Moreover, I do not cease to be the same person just because I have no memory of some of my actions. Butler also argues that identity of person cannot reside in consciousness, because this is never the same any two moments, as we are conscious of different actions. He should have said that we are not conscious of the same events rather than our consciousness is not the same, because he wanted to say that we *are* conscious of being the same person. As we remember actions because we did them, identity of person does not primarily consist in consciousness or memory but in the individual who acts. This was also the view of Hume, who remarked that memory does not so much cause or produce identity of person as *discover* it by acquainting us with the succession of our perceptions.[8]

For Locke, it is enough that I have the memory of some action, even though I did not do it. When we read that George *IV* claimed that he was present at the battle of Waterloo, we also want to know whether this memory of George *IV*'s was a true one. Peter Geach points out that once you inquire about who did an action, you bring in the body as a criterion of identity of person besides memory. Geach says that it is not possible for anyone to remember a deed done by someone else in an earlier existence unless it is already true that the same person turns his mind to the action as did it. So, even if I have Julius Caesar's memory of having crossed the Rubicon, I would not be the same man or person as crossed the Rubicon unless my body were the body that crossed the Rubicon. To be the same person as Caesar, my body would have to have crossed the Rubicon in 49B.C.[9] This is an argument against someone having had a previous existence or being the same person as someone who lived earlier, because there is no identity of body.

Memory does not constitute identity of person, since even when someone loses her memory altogether or has it obliterated, she is still the same person. For someone to say "I have lost my memory", "I" has to be the person whose memory is lost. If I am no longer the person that I used to be, what has happened to the person that was and is no longer, and how has the new person I now am suddenly come into existence without any previous history? Persons are neither extinguished like this, nor do they suddenly spring into being from nowhere.

When Locke claims that the same human being need not be the same person, he drives a wedge between being a human being, or man, and being a person. He says that, if the soul of a prince were to enter the body of a cobbler when the cobbler's soul had left it, it would be the same person but not the same man as the prince.[10] This makes personal identity into something *private*, as everyone would still think it was the cobbler unless the prince told them it was no longer the cobbler but now a prince. If this could happen, it would be more common than it is for people to tell us, like John the Baptist, "I am not the one you think I am".[11]

In ordinary life, however, we normally identify persons by bodily criteria: their face, their manner of walking or fingerprints. When the right suspect has been caught, the counsel for defense does not plead that the court has the same man but not the same person as committed the crime. In law, "offence against the person" means injury to the body. Medical practice too assumes that the same person goes with the same body when the consent of the person is required for an operation to be performed on his or her body. We can alienate all our external possessions but, even though I sell my body to someone else, I cannot make it not be mine, since our bodies are inalienable from ourselves. A body is deemed to have but one owner in its lifetime, whereas it would have several owners if the same man could be several persons.

On Locke's own principle that the same thing has only one beginning of existence, a man could not have a *personal* existence if he could be several persons since only the first person at most could have the same beginning of existence as the man, and he would not have the same beginning of existence as the subsequent persons he became. Alternatively, one could argue, in Locke's favour, that the man has the personal existence of whichever person he is at the time. But, as these persons have different beginnings of existence, he will not be the same man.

Although Locke mainly thinks of one man becoming different persons in succession, he may have provided the idea for Stevenson of one man being two persons by alternation, for he also asks: 'Could we suppose two distinct incommunicable consciousnesses acting in the same body, the one constantly by day, the other by night?'[12] Were Dr Jekyll and Mr Hyde two persons in one body or the same man with a double personality? One way of seeing the answer to this question is to ask yourself whether they shared one memory or had two separate memories. Here the novelist gives us an explicit answer in the voice of Dr Jekyll: 'My two natures had one memory in common.'[13] In the story, Henry Jekyll talks of Edward Hyde, but Hyde never talks about Jekyll. Jekyll brings Hyde into existence by deciding to take the transforming potion, although all that is left at the end is the contorted body that Jekyll turned into during his hours as Mr Hyde.

When we hear of someone who is said to be two 'persons' or to have several 'personalities', it is helpful to talk of character instead of personality. Thus in the famous case of Miss Beauchamp, in 1920's, she was not really four persons but the same person who had four different sets of characteristics.[14] William James observes that alternating personalities are often due to lapses of memory: in passing from one state to another, say an agitated to a calm state, the person has no memory of the previous state.[15] Kathleen Wilkes tells us that the psychiatrist who dealt with Miss Beauchamp thought that he was dealing with only one woman. Wilkes thinks that, as all four personalities shared the same body, we should talk of only one person in this case.[16] Thus Dr Jekyll and Mr Hyde are the same person with two alternating characters rather than one man who is alternately two persons.

Incorporeal Selves

Locke's hypothetical views about the same man becoming different persons imply that a person is something incorporeal, because a person can be transferred to another body, and thus the body is not an essential criterion of personal identity. A similar view of persons as mental rather than bodily beings has been upheld in more recent times by Anthony Quinton. Quinton thought that, if the body is a necessary criterion of personal identity, disembodied existence is impossible. Rather than accept this *reductio ad absurdum*, as it seemed to him, he rejected the premise that leads to it. He begins by noting that there have been three main views about the question: Who is the owner of experiences?

1. The owner of experiences is a spiritual substance, the soul. This was the view of Plato and Descartes.
2. It is the total complex of experiences.
3. It is a body.

Quinton dismisses the first view on the grounds that the identity of a body cannot be due to another substance, for what makes things individual is that they are different pieces of matter. Jenny Teichman too has raised a similar objection. She says that we cannot call souls substances because what individuates souls is that they belong to particular bodies, but the existence and identity of one substance cannot depend on another substance.[17] The answer to Teichman's difficulty is that the soul does not depend on another substance for its existence because, as was said in Chapter Six, it is the soul that makes the body be a substance in the first place: the body is only a substance with its soul. The second reason Quinton gives for saying that the owner of experiences is not a spiritual substance, is that a spiritual substance cannot be used for identifying persons since it is unobservable. As he thus rejects the first view, and the third view because it does not allow the possibility of immortality,

Quinton chooses the second view: the owner of experience is the total complex of experiences. He is not worried by the objection that, if something is identical with its experiences, it cannot be the owner of them.

For Quinton a person is a soul but the soul is not a spiritual substance: rather it is a series of mental states connected by continuity of character and memory that is capable of existing independently of the body.[18] Socrates was a person, but would we say that Socrates was a series of mental states? A person is a soul for Quinton because these mental states constitute a person. It is clear, however, that if a person is just a series of mental states, Quinton is left without any means of explaining the unity of the mental states, so that they are the states of *one* person, since the states make the person. Quinton later tried to remedy this defect by saying that a series of mental states can be conscious of itself provided that recollections of previous tracts of the series are found among the states and experiences of which it is composed.[19]

This is rather like William James' idea that there is a unity of consciousness because thoughts are conscious of thoughts when one thought includes another.[20] James thought that the soul is superfluous, since we only know about it by thoughts, which therefore suffice for explaining consciousness. He replaces the soul with the stream of consciousness, in which every thought knows the previous thought and so on, going all the way back in the series. One wants to know, however, who has these thoughts, for a thought does not think, nor is it a possessor of thoughts, even though it may be a thought of other thoughts. Thoughts need an owner: a thought does not have a thought, although it may contain an earlier thought, but a thinker thinks.[21] One sees that this must be so when one asks how the first thought of the series comes into existence without someone to think it. James, however, took a materialist view, since thought is merely a function of the brain for him. A thought occurs when the brain acts, and 'pulses' of thought correspond to brain processes.[22]

Although Quinton thought bodies are 'intrinsically unimportant' for what makes people unique, and that what is essential for persons is their memory and character, it is worth remarking that what is essential about anything is its essence. Its essence is its nature. But we do not think that human nature consists of memory and character alone. The criteria of personal identity cannot be purely mental, as they are for Quinton, because there are reasons for saying that bodily criteria are also important for the identity of a person. First, it is clear that human beings have corporeal nature and that our bodies partly determine our personality, because we live in the body. Secondly, at least some of our conscious and mental states are of our actions and sensations, both of which involve the body. Indeed we have the experiences that are supposed to constitute the person through having a body. Thirdly, if the body is not essential to what we are, it is hard to understand why we have bodily nature at all.

Having at first rejected the view that the body is a criterion of personal identity, because it seemed to him to preclude the possibility of disembodied existence, ten years later Quinton also rejected disembodied existence altogether.[23] This apparent *volte face* was not, however, inconsistent with his original position, because, if the body is not a criterion of personal identity, you may think that it does not matter which body a person is in as long as it is in some body. So from at first upholding disembodied existence, Quinton now says that a person cannot be disembodied. He thinks that the only reason for believing that not all persons are embodied is the evidence of psychical research. But there are better arguments for the survival of the soul than the claims of psychical research.

Another version of Locke's sort of view of persons was held by H. D. Lewis, who thought that a person is constituted by a set of thoughts, experiences and desires that make him or her distinct from every other person, but that a person is not altogether identical with his or her mental states, because I remain the same person even when my mental states change. I am neither distinct from my thoughts, because these are what make a person for Lewis, nor am I simply identical with them. For Lewis, mental states have a different subject from physical states. The subject of mental states is the self. Thus a self is something other than the body, because it is the subject of mental states and mental states are not material. This makes the self a part of what I am, since I am certainly also a body.

One may make two criticism's of Lewis' dualist view, that *I* am something other than my body. First, a subject is something that acts or reacts. As a human person cannot have experience or sensation without a body, the subject of experiences and mental states cannot be quite distinct from the body. There is the same subject of mental as of physical states. Persons cannot be incorporeal beings, since we do not interact with one another in a purely mental way, as though bodies were merely dummies of other persons.

Secondly, a self cannot be distinct from, or additional to, what I am, when I am a human being and a human being consists of a body. It follows that, as I am a person and I am a human being, a person is not just a self, as Locke and those who follow him think, but a human being. As a human being is a something with a body, a person cannot just be a self or something incorporeal. If a person or self is purely mental or incorporeal, but I have a body, a self is only a part of what I am. But a person or self cannot be a part of what I am, because I am a person. Moreover, the self may be the subject of thoughts but, unless the subject of thoughts and the subject who utters the words which express these thoughts are different, the subject of thoughts is not incorporeal but something with a body. It is one and the same subject who thinks and expresses his or her thoughts by means of the body.

There seems to be much good sense in the argument put forward by Roderick Chisholm. Either I am identical with a substance or I am not. If I am, then I cannot be transferred to another substance, as Locke and others suppose. Or, if I am not identical with a substance, I am two distinct things: a substance (a body) and a person. The question then arises: who or what thinks? Do I think or does a substance think? If I think but I am not identical with a substance, thinking cannot be attributed to a human being, who is something with a body, but only to my 'I', or self, and there are two subjects. Ironically, Locke's view of persons leads to the very dualism that he opposed in Descartes. For I am no more a consciousness than I am just my soul. Locke's fault was that he only thought about persons without asking what *human nature* consists of. When St Thomas Aquinas considers the question whether a disembodied soul is a person, he answers No, because a soul by itself does not have the complete nature of the human species.[24] So Aquinas arrives at his view of a human person by first looking at human nature.

Elizabeth Anscombe thinks that people came to regard persons as incorporeal entities because they looked for something which 'I' names, just as 'Paris' is the name of a city and 'the Seine' the name of a river. As 'I' looks like a name, because it is the word with which everyone refers to him or herself, but 'I' is not the name of any one person, these people think it is the name of an invisible object, a consciousness or self. Thus Locke detached the identity of the self or person from the identity of the human being who says 'I' in expressing his or her thoughts. Anscombe, however, says that 'I' does not name a self, because self-consciousness is not consciousness of a thing called the 'self'; rather it is consciousness that something is true of oneself: that I am sitting in a train travelling along the coast or that a chilly wind is blowing through me.[25]

Anscombe also makes the point that 'person' is not the name of a kind of thing, as say 'fox' or 'hippopotamus' are, but names an *individual* of a certain kind, namely with rational or intelligent nature. Thus human nature can be replicated but persons cannot. A human being is a person because of the kind to which he or she belongs. Since an individual of intelligent nature is a person, the same individual is the same person. Thus the same man cannot become another person, because the same man is the same individual.

As I am neither a consciousness nor just a soul, but I am a person, we require a view of person that takes in the *whole* person. David Braine attempts to meet this requirement with his theory of psycho-physical persons.

The Whole Person

I am a person, but what I am cannot just be my soul or a consciousness, because, as Wittgenstein remarks, "I' am said to be in the same room as my body is in. 'I' clearly refers to my body, since I am in this room; and 'I' is essentially something that is in a place'.[26] Thus the body is an essential criterion of personal identity. It was in order to refute dualism (I am my soul) and materialism (I am just a body) that David Braine introduced his notion of 'psycho-physical' beings. In the first part of his book, *The Human Person*, he corrects Descartes' view of human beings by reminding us of our *animal* nature. In the second part of this book, he combats materialism by showing that human beings are *spirit* as well, because they have an existence that transcends the body. His aim, however, is to show that we are spirit without bringing in the soul, because the soul seems to take us back into dualism.[27] In this section, I want to see whether Braine is successful in his attempt to show that we have a transcendent existence without bringing in the soul.

Braine rightly maintains that we have to treat human beings as *wholes*, because we cannot separate the mental from the physical. Neither dualism nor materialism can provide an adequate view of human beings, because intention belongs to physical movement *internally*, although it is not itself physical. Braine argues that not all causation is physical, because intention is internal to action but it is not anything studied by the biologist or neuro-physiologist in describing what happens when we act, even though it accompanies our actions. Braine remarks that our actions do not have a purely mechanical explanation, because memory and thought are causes of action. The best explanations of our actions are often mental ones: choice, desire, judgement. But the dualist view is equally wrong, because perception is not merely mental but involves bodily organs. A human being is a unity, since perception and intention belong to one another integrally. Unless we have this unity, intention would be divorced from the body that perceives and acts. Because of this unity of the physical and intentional in human beings and higher animals, Braine calls them *psychophysical* beings. What makes something a psycho-physical being is that it manifests a kind of life and behaviour, which is not explicable in purely physical terms.

What distinguishes human beings from other animal is that they are also spirit. To have spirit means, for Braine, to have an existence which transcends the body. His key for demonstrating this is language. He chooses language rather than thinking or understanding, because this is the particular way in which the intellectual life of bodily beings like ourselves manifests itself. Our intellectual activity is not wordless contemplation, as it is for angels, but consists of judgements that we express in words. Language is 'expressive' for Braine because thinking is not itself the operation of a bodily organ, although thought is given bodily expression. Thus thinking is not an activity of the body, although thinking and speaking go together. Language shows that we have an existence transcending the body, because the *understanding* of words and speech cannot be states of a bodily organ or material system.[28] There are, for example, no mechanical rules for understanding new sentences that we have never met before. Understanding language is also not mechanical, because we do not use words without also reflecting on them. Nor is the understanding of words and sentences correlated with states of the nervous system. Thought has a bodily expression, but no neural activity corresponds with the thoughts themselves.

Since language expresses thought and there are no words without concepts, Braine does not explain *why* we have an existence that transcends the body unless he can also show how it is possible for us to have understanding and thought when these are not the power of a bodily organ, for they must be the power of something; but Braine does not say of what, since he does not want to bring in the soul. Braine says that thinking and understanding are done by the whole person indivisibly. This may well be true, but if we are to avoid materialism some further explanation is required. Without the soul, Braine shows at best *that* human beings have a transcendent existence, because they have language, but not also *why*.

Braine leaves two further questions unanswered. First, how does this transcendent existence come into existence, because this can only be through something higher than the body? Braine leaves no room in his theory for the creation of the soul. Secondly, as a human being has a single existence, how does this existence continue after this life unless there is something else besides the body to be the bearer of it? Braine is caught in a dilemma, because he says that the existence of the soul just is the existence of the human being.[29] If this is so, either the soul ceases to exist when the human being dies and his existence does not transcend the body or, if the existence of the human being continues, we have to say what is the bearer of this existence after the body dies. Braine is reluctant to admit that it is the soul, for he says 'One could say one is a soul, but not as if the soul were a sort of thing.'[30] If the soul is not some sort of thing, it must be something else that survives and continues to bear the transcendent existence. To escape his dilemma, Braine resorts to saying that when one dies one is neither a body nor a soul but a 'deprived person'. But what is a person when he or she has been deprived of the body by death except a soul? Since Braine leaves out the soul, he only secures transcendence for this life. If, however, our existence is truly transcendent, then we do not just know things in a higher than material way in this life but we also survive the body.

Braine's theory of psycho-physical beings also raises the question of how we can call anything psychological unless there is such a thing as the soul. It is quite common for philosophers to call verbs like perceive, remember, know, intend 'psychological', but even if one says these are not material properties of a person, there seems no reason why we should call them *psychological* unless a person is not just a body but also has a soul. Thus Braine avoids dualism at the expense of not being able to show that we have an existence which transcends this life, or indeed why we are spirit, unless he can also explain why we have understanding, which language presupposes, when it is not the power of a bodily organ.

. We have seen that a person is not something incorporeal like a soul, a consciousness, or a series of mental states, but that the body is an essential part of our identity as persons. On the other hand, we have seen that Braine's attempt to show the unity of the human person without the soul is unable to explain why we have understanding or an existence that is not just transcendent for this life. Our concept of the human person, then, requires the body and the soul. Without the soul we do not survive, for no bearer of our existence is left after the body dies. On the other hand, if only the soul survives, the human *person* does not remain. Thus the continued existence of the person requires the resurrection of the body as well as the immortality of the soul. It is to these two questions that we now turn.

NOTES

1. *An Essay Concerning Human Understanding* (*Essay* for short) Bk II c. 27, 4.
2. *Ibid.* II c. 1, 19.
3. *Ibid.* II c. 27, 9.
4. *Ibid.* II c. 27, 26.
5. *Ibid.* II c. 27, 13-14.
6. *The Analogy of Religion* (1736 Macmillan 1900) Dissertation I 10, p284.
7. *Ibid.* Dissertation I 3, p280.
8. *A Treatise of Human Nature* I iv 6 (Selby-Bigge 262).
9. *God and the Soul* (Routledge & Kegan Paul 1979) 4.
10. *Essay* II 27, 15.
11. *Acts* 13, 25.
12. *Essay* II 27, 23
13. *Dr Jekyll and Mr Hyde* (Penguin Classics) 79.
14. B. Williams, *Problems of Self* (Cambridge 1973) 18.
15. *Principles of Psychology* I 379.
16. *Real People* (*Oxford* 1988) 119.
17. *The Mind and Soul* (Routledge & Kegan Paul 1974) 17.
18. The Soul, *Journal of Philosophy* (59) 1962, 403.
19. *The Nature of Things* (Routledge & Kegan Paul 1973) 99.
20. *Principles of Psychology* I 339f.
21. *Ibid.* I 371.
22. *Ibid.* I 401, 345.
23. *The Nature of Things* 100.
24. *ST* 1a 29, 1 ad 5.

25 The First Person (1974), in *Collected Philosophical Papers*
    (Blackwell 1981) vol. II 25.
26 *Philosophical Remarks* 55.
27 *The Human Person* (Duckworth 1993) 9, 541.
28 *Ibid.* 348.
29 *Ibid.* 541.
30 *Ibid.* 540.

10

IMMORTALITY AND RESURRECTION

In the past many of those who believed in life after death thought that the immortality of the soul alone sufficed. If, however, the body is an essential criterion of personal identity, that is, of who I am, which we saw to be so in the previous chapter, then the immortality of the soul will not by itself be enough for the continuation of a human person, but the resurrection of the body will also be required. Now the pendulum has swung the other way: from thinking uppermost of the immortality of the soul we now meet writers who teach the resurrection of the body without the immortality of the soul. If there is only a resurrection but the soul is not immortal, it is not apparent that the same person will be raised up again, for unless something of us remains in existence after death, we will have a new beginning of existence, but the same thing has only one beginning of existence. In this chapter, I first want to give reasons for believing in the immortality of the soul, which is widely disbelieved today, and, secondly, to show that belief in the resurrection of the body without the immortality of the soul, apart from being contrary to Christian tradition, fails to secure the resurrection of the same person. There may well be no immortality without hope of the resurrection, and the resurrection cannot be demonstrated by reason, but it can be shown that faith in the resurrection meets what reason requires if the human person is to receive complete existence again after this life. As Peter Geach has said, the doctrine of the resurrection is the only intelligible one about survival, since an immortal soul alone would not be the permanent survival of the whole person. Geach argues that the possibility of survival requires the capacity for renewed human life, since the identity of the soul depends on its capacity for reunion with its body.[1]

The Possibility of Immortality

The main objection to belief in the immortality of the soul is that the mind seems to depend on the brain, since the physical state of the brain clearly affects our ability to think. When the brain is tired, it is more difficult to think; injuries to the brain alter a person's power to think. The Cambridge philosopher John Ellis Mᶜ Taggart (1866-1925) said about this objection:

> With regard to the connexion of the brain with thought, the chief evidence for it appears to be that diseases or mutilations of the brain affect the course of thought. But this does not prove that, even while a man has a brain, his thoughts are directly connected with it.

Mᶜ Taggart thought that far from the soul depending on the brain, the mind might well be open to new ways of perception when it is freed from the limitation of the body.

> Even if the brain is essential to thought while we have bodies, it would not follow that when we ceased to have brains we could not think without them. The same argument applies here as with the organs of sense. It might be that the present inability of the self to think except in connexion with the body was a limitation which was imposed by the presence of the body, and which vanished with it.[2]

It does not follow that, because we cannot think without the brain functioning well in this present life, we could not think without the body, since we could have another mode of knowing in another mode of existence. Although thinking is accompanied by physical processes, this does not necessarily mean that it is the power of a bodily organ. Thinking depends on the body for its data, but it goes beyond the information transmitted from the senses to the brain when we have abstract thought. The mind seems anyway to have a certain independence of the body, since thoughts cannot be correlated one to one with events in the brain. The mind's connection with the body in this life does not show that we could not think apart from the body. As Mᶜ Taggart says:

> It does not follow because a self which has a body cannot get its data except in connexion with the body, that it would be impossible for a self without a body to get its data in some other way. It may be just the existence of the body which makes these other ways impossible at present.[3]

One of the difficulties people have in believing in the immortality of the soul is that they are tied, like H. H. Price, to the idea that our knowledge in the next life will just consist in images of things in this life, and so the next world will consist of memories of this world. They do not see that, as the mind is immaterial, there could also be an immaterial reality, which we do not directly apprehend in this life but will be able to know beyond this world. Price thought that the next life consists of having images and that this world of images is a real world, because the images themselves are not imaginary, for we experience them. But if the next world is an imaginary one, there will be as many worlds as minds imagining. The centre of this world, Price thought, would be images of one's body. But the images of a body that no longer existed could not be anything that *acted*.[4]

We notice that Mᶜ Taggart prefers to talk about the 'self' instead of the soul. Since he did not think that the identity of a man throughout his bodily life is the identity of his soul, he thought that speaking of the immortality of the soul does not make clear the identity of a person between this life and the next.[5] He did not think that our identity in this life is of the soul because it seemed to him that, if a man has a soul, he is something else, namely a body. And if he is a body that has a soul, when the body dies he ceases to exist and the soul that survives, because immortal, would be something other than himself. So he replaced the soul with the self, but to do this

leads into dualism, as we noted in the previous chapter, because
it makes the self a part of what I am, for the self is quite distinct
from the body but I also have a body. In the same way, when Fr
Edmund Hill O.P. proposes that we replace soul with 'self' or
'person', he runs into the very dualism that he strongly opposes,
because he does not see that this raises as many difficulties as it
is meant to solve.[6]

M[c] Taggart also pointed out that natural science supports
rather than disproves the possibility of immortality, because
nothing is annihilated in nature, but when something ceases to
exist it is only the compound of the elements that is dissolved,
not the elements themselves. In our case, it is the compound
being of body and soul.

Survival of the Individual

Aristotle thought that it would only be possible for the soul
to exist separately from the body if it has an activity which
affects the soul alone but that, if thinking is merely a form
of imagination or only occurs with imagination, not even
thinking could exist apart from the body.[7] We can show that
the mind is not just the imagination in two ways. First, the
imagination only has images neutrally, so to speak; it does not
make judgements about them, whether they are true or false.
For example, I may have the image of a winged horse, but it
is with another faculty than the imagination that I judge this
image not to be of anything real. Secondly, if the mind were
no more than the imagination, I would not have self-reflection,
because when I reflect on my activity of seeing, for example, I
do not have another image of seeing itself besides the image of
the thing that I see. Thus reflecting on one's seeing is something
other than seeing. As I know that I see at the same time as I see
something, but I do not have an image of seeing as I have of the
object seen, not all thinking can be just imagination.

As Aristotle calls the soul the form of the body, it seems
that the soul could not exist apart from that of which it is
the form but must go out of existence with the body. It is not
clear what Aristotle himself thought about the survival of the
individual soul, since he says the mind comes from outside

and is something 'divine'. When he says that the mind (*nous*) is separate 'and this alone is immortal', he may have meant that what survives is part of some separately existing mind.[8] This is how his Arab commentators, Avicenna(980-1037) and Averroes (1126-1198) understood him. When Aristotle says that the mind is separate, they thought he meant there is a universal mind that exists separately from us and in which we all share. Aquinas, however, argued against Averroes that the text of Aristotle makes it clear that he did not mean there is a universal mind that exists separately from us but that our mind is separate in the sense that it is not the power of a bodily organ, not separate from us in its existence.[9] Aquinas saw that the doctrine of a universal mind, in which we all share, undermines belief in reward and punishment in the next life, without which we cannot see that justice will eventually be done, because it would mean that when I think, an external mind thinks in me. My actions would not then be my own, for which I could receive reward or punishment, since I would not be responsible for them if I were not moved by my own mind but some external, universal mind.

One still meets people today, including natural scientists, who think that there is just one mind, in which we all share. Schrödinger, for example, thought that there is one consciousness that is like a great canvas on which we each have a separate patch but we overlap in a shared view of the world. There is one view of the world, without which natural science would not be possible, because there is one consciousness, he thought.[10] Schrödinger came to this view as the answer to his question: 'How does one picture of the world crystallize out of many minds?' He thought there is only one consciousness because we all only know consciousness in the singular. If there were only one consciousness, however, we would all be one human being.

There have been three ways of solving the difficulty that Aristotle's theory of the soul presents for its immortality.
1. The soul can survive, but only because it is re-embodied. This is re-incarnation.

2. The soul cannot survive on its own, but only by becoming part of a universal soul.

3. The soul can survive when separated from the body, because it is subsistent.

The first view preserves the individuality of the soul but sacrifices the identity of the person, since the soul does not keep the same body. As Anthony Kenny has said, the soul is only *my* soul because it is the soul of this body. The soul that is the form of the body can only be the form of *one* body. Re-incarnation regards the body as a mere house for the soul rather than an integral part of the human person. It also means that either one soul has several unrelated histories in different bodies at different times, or its several lives belong to the history of one person, but we could not be sure that, when we meet someone, he or she is not the same person as someone who lived in the past. Re-incarnation and resurrection are exclusive of one another, because the resurrection is rising to a new kind of life, never to die again; it is not returning to the same kind of life.

The second view sacrifices both the individuality of the soul and the identity of the person, since the soul is merged into a greater one. This view is part of Buddhism.

The third view is the solution of St Thomas Aquinas. When he adopted Aristotle's theory that the soul is the form of the body, he needed to modify it, since it is not clear that Aristotle allowed for the survival of the individual soul. As mentioned above, he may have thought that the part of the soul that survives, the intellect (*nous*), was part of a universal mind. Aquinas showed that the soul can survive on its own, because it is a special kind of form, a *subsistent* form, as it has an activity which is not the function of a bodily organ, namely thinking. We should not be surprised that the human soul is a special kind of form, since human beings occupy a special position in the universe, standing on the border between the material and immaterial, as we uniquely consist of body and spirit. On the one hand, we gather knowledge from material things; on the other, we can think of them generally, which is not how they exist in matter, for they are particular.

> Inasmuch as the soul has an activity transcending matter, it is raised above the body and is not dependent on it. But inasmuch as it is made to acquire immaterial knowledge from material things, it is not complete in its nature apart from union with the body.[11]

Immaterial knowledge is to have the general concepts of things.

The human soul is united to the body as its form, but it is also raised above it by its power of knowing things in an immaterial way. Thus the human soul is not tied to the body for all its activities but *transcends* the body. The souls of animals are tied to the body for all their activities, so cannot survive separately from the body. The human soul depends on the body for the *data* of thinking but can operate on its own, because the exercise of the mind's power in thinking *on* these data is not a function of a bodily organ. Victor Brezik argues in the following way that the distinctive powers of the human soul show that it is subsistent. Forms either depend on matter and are not subsistent or they are independent of matter and are subsistent. Forms that depend on matter do not have an operation of their own; but the human soul has an activity which is not that of a bodily organ, so it is subsistent.[12] The soul is *above* the body, because we can reflect *on* our perceiving and thinking. For Aquinas, the human soul is subsistent and the form of the body. For Plato and Descartes the soul is subsistent but not the form of the body. They cannot, therefore, explain the unity of the body and soul if the body has another form than the soul (assuming that every body has a form of some sort).

Anthony Kenny accuses Aquinas of making a power into an hypostasis when he calls the human soul a subsistent form. Kenny's argument goes like this: if the soul is 'this particular thing' (*hoc aliquid*), as Aquinas says it is, but a hand or foot does not subsist by itself, why does not the soul just exist like a hand or foot but also subsist? And if a human being thinks by his soul as he sees by his eye, as Aquinas also says, should he not say that only a human being subsists but not the soul, just as an eye does not subsist?[13] Kenny overlooks two points in his argument.

First, the soul is not a 'this something' just like any part of the body, because it is related to the *whole* of the body as its form. Secondly, seeing depends on the bodily organ of the eye, but the human soul has an activity that is not dependent on the body, namely thinking of things in a general, immaterial way. Aquinas would only be guilty of making a power into a hypostasis if he thought that the soul were a power. But the soul is not a power; it is the *actuality*, for it is what makes the body a living one. A hand or foot cannot exist on its own when separated from the body, because they no longer have their form, but the soul can because it *is* the form of a human being.

Aquinas remarks that it does not follow that, when the body perishes, the soul also perishes, because what ceases to exist is the composite whole of body and soul. But this does not prevent one of its parts from surviving. A composite thing ceases to exist when it loses its form, but if this form is itself subsistent, because it has an activity of its own, it can remain in existence.

One might argue that there is no need for the human form to be subsistent so that it can survive, as long as we are raised up again, because a piece of furniture can be dismantled, its parts stored away and then be restored. Then we have the same table or chair again, although its form did not exist in the meantime. A piece of furniture, however, is an artefact and artefacts are not like living things. Artefacts, like tables and clocks, have an accidental form, because their parts can exist intact on their own when the table or clock no longer exists. But a living thing has a *substantial* form, because its parts only have their form when they are united to the whole body. Thus a living thing can only be restored if its form remains in existence, for its parts do not remain intact on their own but decay. As we saw in Chapter Three, the identity of a living thing is of its *form*, since its matter is continually being changed. A closer analogy for the resurrection of the body than restoring a table would be to suppose that the parts of the table decayed into dust while being stored. If it were possible to restore the table from the dust of its parts, would it be the same table or a new table with a new form? I think the latter. Likewise, the same human being is not raised up again unless his or her form remains in existence because it is a subsistent form.

Resurrection without Immortality

Nonetheless, it is quite common now for writers to profess that the Christian hope is of a resurrection alone without any immortality of the soul. This view can be found in Thomas Hobbes (1588-1679), who based it on *Job* 14, 7-12: when a tree is cut down it sprouts again, but when a man dies he has no life until he rises again.

> That the Soul of man is in its own nature Eternal, and a living Creature independent of the Body, or that any meer man is Immortal, otherwise than by the Resurrection in the last day (except Enos and Elias) is a doctrine not apparent in Scripture.... Therefore where Job saith, man riseth not till the Heavens be no more, it is all one as if he said, the Immortal Life (and Soul and Life in Scripture do usually signifie the same thing) beginneth not in man, till the Resurrection and day of Judgement; and hath for cause not his specificall nature.[14]

If nothing of us remains in existence when we die but trees sprout again, we are worse off than trees, although human beings are thought to represent the highest point of life in the visible world.

Hobbes partly rests his argument on the equivalence of soul for life in the New Testament. He is followed in this by many Scripture scholars today. It can be shown, however, that *psuche* (soul) is not always to be translated as 'life' in the New Testament. For example, when Christ says: 'Do not fear those who kill the body but cannot kill the soul (*psuchen*); rather fear Him who is able to kill soul and body in hell'.[15] As this saying supposes that it is possible to kill the body without killing the soul, it implies that the soul can survive. But this point is quite lost if soul is translated as life here; rather it is rendered meaningless, because it would be like saying, 'Do not fear those who can kill the body but cannot kill the life'. To kill the body is to destroy its life. Christ implies that the soul can survive, because he goes on to say, 'rather fear Him who is able to kill soul and body in hell'. As the soul is not killed in hell in this life, it must be in an existence after this life. Biblical scholars point out that there is no express mention of the immortality of the soul in the New Testament. One reason for this may be that the immortality of the soul was something already believed by pagans in the ancient world. St Paul, however, also counts immortality as one of the new things 'brought to light through the Gospel'.[16]

According to John Polkinghorne, the Christian hope is death and resurrection, not an intrinsic immortality. Polkinghorne says, 'We are a complex information - carrying pattern which persists through all the changes of material constituents and which by its very persistence expresses the true continuity of my person, that person is the meaning of the soul'.[17] Polkinghorne appears to combine two quite different views here: the soul is the pattern of material constituents and the soul is my person. Although he takes his view to be that of the soul as the form of the body, it should be carefully distinguished from Aquinas' view, since Polkinghorne thinks that this pattern is dissolved with the disintegration of the body but Aquinas thought that the human form survives. Polkinghorne believes that the pattern made up of material constituents will be recreated at the resurrection, when the pattern dissolved by death will be reconstructed.[18] As the soul is a material form for Polkinghorne, since it is the pattern of material constituents, the mind too must be material in his view. Although he finds it 'a coherent hope' that the information-bearing pattern of our bodies will be remembered by God between death and resurrection and be recreated by him in a final act of resurrection, the same person cannot be raised up if he goes out of existence altogether, for this would be a totally new beginning of existence. As Polkinghorne says that the persistence of the complex information-bearing pattern that is my soul expresses the continuity of my person in this life, by the same argument he ought to require the persistence of something between death and resurrection, so that the *same* person can be resurrected. There is no identity without some continuity of existence.

Like Polkinghorne, the English Dominican father, Simon Tugwell, says that the Christian hope is of the resurrection alone. Tugwell's special concern is to preserve the significance of death; what difference does death make if our souls continue to be conscious after all? Tugwell appeals to an old argument, which he thinks could be given another run for its money: the dead are still alive to God, for he 'is not God of the dead but of the living, for all are alive to him'.[19] All that is necessary for us to remain in existence between our death and resurrection is that we are in some way still alive to God. We have no need to appeal to some 'Deep Fact', by which Tugwell presumably means a substantial soul, since the Creator guarantees the identity of the person raised up. In order to establish the identity of the person that will be raised up, Tugwell resorts to saying that God creates, recreates, a life-story and identifies someone as the person whose story it is. Tugwell recognizes that some memory is required for this to be possible, but he says that no more is needed than God could produce by creating someone's memories afresh. He explains this with the help of an analogy: God is like an artist and we are like works of art shaped by the divine artist. Tugwell asks us to imagine a drawing that begins as the drawing of a giraffe and, as a result of many alteration, turns into a drawing of a rhinoceros. Tugwell thinks that this is still the same drawing, although it no longer looks like the original. I would say that whether it remains the same drawing depends on whether it is on the same piece of paper. It is only the same drawing if the same piece of paper is used throughout, but if successive drawings are done on one new piece of paper after another, we get different drawings. But as the lines of a drawing do not exist on their own, likewise a life-story or set of memories cannot exist on its own. As the lines must exist on a piece of paper, so memories do not remain unless something of the person still exists. Tugwell would say that God keeps them in existence, but this is no easier to suppose than that God keeps the soul in existence. As we noted in the previous chapter, memory is not a sufficient criterion for identity of person.

Tugwell also argues that a continuity of God's creative purpose for each one of us is enough to ensure the continuity of the same person, since all that matters is that we eventually become the person God intends us to be. But how are we to account for those who by their own free choice resist God and fail to become what God intended them to be? God does not make anyone into what he intends him or her to be irrespectively of the life he or she has lived in this world. If a person has to be created entirely afresh, because nothing has remained in existence between the end of this life and the resurrection, an identical person will not be raised up because nothing raised up will have been through the experiences and circumstances that make us the persons we are in this life. Even though the final shaping of us may be God's work as he refines us, the final product must have some continuity of existence with what existed in this life. After all, when a potter reshapes a pot, he still uses the same lump of clay. We cannot even speak of God recreating a person's memories unless the same person is raised up, because they would not be memories of things done by that person. Thus Tugwell's theory presupposes the identity of the person rather than explains how it will be restored at the resurrection.

Tugwell's view of the soul seems to be that it is no more than the 'contents of someone's mental life'. This view is little removed from that of Hume: the mind is a bundle of perceptions or complex of mental states. What matters for Tugwell is not the immortality of the soul but an after-life rather than the lasting extinction of the person. For the *same* person to be raised up, there has to be some continuity of existence between death and resurrection. If we are raised up when nothing of us has remained in existence, the same person will not be raised up. Tugwell seems to recognize this, since he adds: 'What we perceive as a break in the continuity of their existence is not an interruption of their existence in the sight of God'.[20] One can only say that a break in the existence of anything is also a break in the sight of God, since he sees all things as they are in reality.

With Tugwell, one could say that we have no need to suppose that the soul continues to exist after death, since all that is required is that the dead are alive to God. But nothing is alive unless it is active in some way, and for something to be able to act it must be subsistent; otherwise, we are not using the words 'alive' and 'to live' in their proper sense but equivocally. So unless something of us survives when we die we are not even alive to God.

Unless the soul survives as something subsistent, several Catholic doctrines are undermined. First, if the saints in heaven are able to hear our prayers when we pray to them, they must be subsistent. Presumably, God does not answer the prayers we make to the saints unless they also know that they have been invoked, if they are truly instrumental in bringing about what we pray to them for. But they cannot be active or instrumental in bringing about the answer to our prayers unless something of them remains in existence.

If we are to talk of those who have died in the love of God as either enjoying the vision of God in heaven or being refined in Purgatory, they must be something in-between death and resurrection. The idea of Purgatory is one that can be grasped by reason, for the atheist Mc Taggart thought that even the best of men may not be ready to enter heaven straightaway on dying but would need some further purification.[21] Only he supposed that we are purified by repeated lives on earth rather than in a state of purification beyond this life. But we can decide which of these alternatives is more reasonable, because if we return to successive lives in this world, our life would lose much of its purpose, since it would not matter so much what we did in one life, for one could always amend it in another or the next time round. As this requires that we die several times over, death would no longer be 'the undiscovered country from whose bourn no traveller returns'.[22] Purgatory, then, is a least as reasonable a belief as re-incarnation. But no one is in heaven or in Purgatory unless they have charity. There must, however, be a subject of the virtue of charity. Nor can those in Purgatory long for heaven, or the blessed in heaven await the resumption of their bodies, unless they are something subsistent, since longing and expecting are activities. One could say that the subject is the person, but this leads to dualism as it makes the person something other than the body and soul. If the person survives before the resurrection, the resurrection of the body seems unnecessary. But it is just the resurrection of the body that Simon Tugwell wants to preserve.

If nothing of the person survives after death, the same person cannot be raised up again, because the resurrection is not like making a replica of the person. Aquinas points out that it is not the same for the soul to go out of existence as it is for the body, because a body resolves into its material constituents, which go on existing, but there is nothing for a soul to resolve into: it either survives or goes out of existence altogether. The resurrection of the body is not like making an exact replica of a bronze statue whose matter has been melted down and recast in the same form. This is not the same statue but a new one with another individual form, Aquinas says. At the resurrection, however, the same person will be raised up because the body will be restored with the same form as it had in this life. It is possible for the body to be restored to the same form, because the soul remains in existence. This is because the human soul is a subsistent form.[23] The soul cannot be restored, or raised up again, as the body can out of material elements, since the only way that the human soul can be brought into existence is by being created, because it is immaterial. The same soul cannot be recreated; it would have to be an entirely new soul with a new beginning of existence.

Immediate Resurrection

Another way of arguing that there is no need for the immortality of the soul is to say that there is no gap between death and resurrection, because there is no time in the next life. Thus there is no gap which needs to be bridged. One might as well say that, since God is outside time and sees all things simultaneously, for things are only present to him, there is no real gap between events in this world. There is as much difficulty about gaps between events in history for the timelessness of God as there is about the gap between death and resurrection in the next world, but we do not therefore say that the gaps in history are not real. As we know that there are gaps between events in history, unless you deny the reality of time altogether, so there is a gap between death and resurrection. What is a gap for us is one in the sight of God too, for he sees all things as they really are. If, as orthodox Christian faith believes, the resurrection will take place at the end of time, there is an interval between death and resurrection. We have good reason to think that the resurrection of the dead has not yet happened, because we know that the bodies of the dead are still in their graves.

An American scholar, Montague Brown, says that we know the soul is immaterial, and so incorruptible, and that body and soul have a *natural* unity. Thus the immortality of the soul requires the resurrection of the body. He then goes on to argue against the soul existing on its own, which is what we mean by the immortality of the soul, because he thinks that, as the soul on its own is not a human person, there is a break in the continuity of the person, so that it will not be the same 'me' that is resurrected as lives now.[24] On St Thomas' view, that a disembodied soul is not a person because it lacks the complete nature of a human being, if there is a gap between death and resurrection when the soul alone survives, we have to say that we cease to be persons or that we have an incomplete existence. For this reason, it is better to say with John Haldane that we are 'fragments' of persons.[25] Montague Brown prefers to save the identity of person by denying any discontinuity of person, because there is no gap between death and resurrection. There is no more difficulty, however, about the same *person* being resurrected in spite of the discontinuity of person than there is about the same human being restored, as long as something of us remains in existence. Although we only have a human person with the body, the same person can be raised up again as long as the soul survives, because the body gets its existence from the soul. All that is required is that the body is restored to the existence of the soul. Montague Brown's argument does not raise an insurmountable objection to the possibility of the same 'me' being resurrected, because the discontinuity of the person is not discontinuity of existence altogether. How the body can be restored to its soul is the question that we now have to consider in the last part of this chapter.

What Sort of Body?

The body can be restored to the existence of the same person, since the body gets its existence from the soul. As Aquinas notes, the same person will be raised up, because the body will be restored to the existence of the same person as had it in this life.[26] This is the existence of the soul. For the body to be restored to the existence of the same person, it must have had the existence of only one person. This rules out the possibility of the same man becoming another person. It was not a matter of indifference for Aquinas, as it was for Locke, which parcel of matter a soul goes into.[27] The difficulty is how the soul retains the same individual existence when forms of the same kind are only individuated by being the forms of different lumps of matter. The soul gets its individuality from being in one body. As it does not perish with the body, so neither does it lose its individuality when separated from the body.

> Although its (the soul's) individuation depends contingently on a body from its beginning, since it does not acquire individual existence except in a body, of which it is the completion, its individuality however does not perish when the body is destroyed. Since it exists of itself, through acquiring individual existence as the form of this particular body it always remains individual in its existence.[28]

Although the soul is no longer with the body that individuated it, it remains individual because it remains in existence, and its existence is different from that of any other soul because it was in another body from any other soul.[29] This is Aquinas' solution of the difficulty that Quinton raised about how disembodied souls remain individual when forms are individuated by different lumps of matter. The soul remains individual, because it belonged to one body. The soul keeps this individual existence as it persists with the same existence. At first, Aquinas only made the individuality of the separated soul *retro*spective, because it *had* been in a particular body. Later he thought its individuality is also *pro*spective, because it retains the capacity for reunion with this body in the future. From this point of view, if one grants that the soul is immortal, the resurrection is to be expected since the soul has a *natural* inclination to be united with its body: 'so the human soul remains in its existence when separated from the body, having an aptitude and natural inclination for union with the body'.[30]

I have so far said that the same soul remains in existence. But how can the same body be raised up again? This is not so difficult to imagine when bodies are raised up from their graves as it is for bodies that have been burnt and scattered as ashes, blown to pieces in an explosion or eaten by wild beasts. Will the body that decays be reformed out of the same particles of matter? Does the body of a particular person require the same matter or just the same configuration of matter? Is it possible to restore even numerically the same body from new particles of matter? As a person retains numerically the same body in this life, although all its matter is changed, because new matter becomes part of a continuous body with the same form, it need not be a body with the very same bits of matter to be the same body that is raised up. All that is needed is that the body we each get back at the resurrection is unmistakably our own body, which is quite distinct from everyone else's. We see that in this life everyone's body expresses just this one personality. Even before we discern the features of someone's face we can recognize who he or she is from a distance just by their distinctive manner of walking and overall shape. Thus all that is required for the same body to be raised up is that it expresses, or embodies, this unique person. In re-incarnation, the same person has several bodies; so the body does not express just this one person, for the bodies differ.

St Thomas says that it does not need to be the same matter for the same human being or person to rise again, just as there is one fire, although ever new logs of wood, which are the matter of the fire, are added to it.

Thus for numerically the same human being to rise again it is not required that anything in him materially for the whole time of his life be resumed, but only as much of it as suffices to complete the right quantity.[31]

What matters for the same person to be raised up is that a body of the same *nature* will be raised up, otherwise it will not be a human *person* that is raised up. Although people find it hard to imagine how we could have material bodies in the next life, an analogy used by St Thomas helps here. He compares the body with stained glass: the risen body will differ from our present body in its state but not in its being matter, just as stained glass is still the same matter although it is quite dull and opaque when seen from outside but translucent and brilliant when seen from inside with the light shinning through it.[32] In the same way, we can have a body of the same nature when it is raised up, although it will be in another state. St Paul describes the difference between our present body and the risen one thus: what is sown is a natural body (*soma psuchikon*, literally an *ensouled* body), but what is raised up is a spiritual body (*soma pneumatikon*).[33] A spiritual body is still a body, but it is one that is entirely subject to the Spirit. Unless we rise with bodies of the same nature, we will only be human beings equivocally; it will not be '*me*', a human being, that is raised up.

We may think of the transformation of the body in glory in a physical way, as matter has another aspect when radiated by strong light. But the risen bodies of the blessed will first of all be transformed because the glory which their souls reflect will shine through their bodies. Even in this life we talk of someone being 'radiant with joy'. One may imagine the transformation of the risen body by an analogy with the radiation of matter, but the risen body will be more transformed by the light that the soul reflects than by any merely physical change. The soul is more disposed to reflect the light of God's glory the more it has of the virtues. All shall rise again, for all human beings have the same nature; but only the bodies of the blessed will shine with glory. 'There will be a resurrection of both the just and unjust'.[34]

I began this chapter by countering some of the arguments that prevent people from allowing that the soul is immortal. But the immortality of the soul is not by itself sufficient for the survival of the person, since the body too is an essential criterion of a person's identity. So the same person does not have perpetual existence unless the soul eventually resumes its body. Some argue, however, that there is no need for the soul to be immortal, since the resurrection of the body is the hope of Christians and this is enough for the person to be restored. The resurrection, however, requires the immortality of the soul, because there has to be some continuity of existence between death and resurrection for the *same* person to be raised up. As this is not the existence of the body, which dies, it must be of the soul. The alternative is that we are raised up straightaway after dying, but this is contrary to Christian tradition. The soul is immortal because it is subsistent, that is, it can exist on its own because it has an independent activity. Thus neither the immortality of the soul nor the resurrection alone is sufficient for the permanent existence of the *same* person, but each requires the other; they are not alternatives but go together.

Although there may be no reason to hold that the soul is immortal without hope of the resurrection, but the resurrection is something known only by faith, nonetheless the resurrection meets the requirement of reason, for there is no permanent survival of the human *person* without the resurrection of the body. The immortality of the soul alone does not secure the perpetual existence of the person, since the soul by itself is not a human person. As Aquinas says, 'if only my soul is saved, I am not saved, nor is any other human being', for I am not just my soul.[35] But without the immortality of the soul the same person is not raised up, because if the soul too goes out of existence, there is a new beginning of existence. What is raised up is what dies. This is not the soul but the body. The same soul cannot be raised up because human souls only come into existence by being created. Although the immortality of the soul alone would be some kind of permanent existence, it would not be of the complete person. Nor would immortality of the soul alone be victory over death without the resurrection of the body as well, for death is only truly overcome if that which dies, the body, is raised up again.

NOTES

[1] *God and the Soul* (Routledge & Kegan Paul 1969) 28.

[2] *Immortality and Pre-Existence* (Arnold London 1915) 60.

[3] *Ibid.* 58.

[4] Survival and the Idea of 'Another World', *Brain and Mind* ed. J.R. Smythies (London 1965) 7.

[5] *Loc cit* 10.

[6] *Being Human* (Chapman 1984) 105f.

[7] *De Anima* I c.1 403a 10.

[8] *Ibid* III c.5 430 a 25.

[9] *De Unitate Intellectus* 14.

[10] *What is Life? Mind and Matter* (Cambridge 1967) 49, 98.

[11] *Quaestiones de Anima* q.1 end of central reply.

[12] The Descent of Man according to Thomas Aquinas, *Thomistic Papers* ed. V. Brezik (Houstan 1984) vol. 1 90.

[13] *Aquinas on the Mind* (Routledge 1993) 135.

[14] *Leviathan* Pt III c.38 (ed. W.G. Pogson Smith 350).

[15] *Matthew* 10, 28.

[16] *2 Tim* 1, 10.

[17] *Science and Creation* (S.P.C.K. 1988) 72.

[18] *One World* (S.P.C.K. 1986) 77.

[19] Luke 20, 38.

[20] *Human Immortality* (Darton, Longman & Todd 1990) 160.

[21] *Immortality and Pre-Existence* 80.

[22] Hamlet Act 3 sc.1 (bourn means boundary)

[23] *Quodlibet* XI q.6, 6 ad 3.

[24] Aquinas on the Resurrection of the Body, *The Thomist* 56 (1992) 196.

[25] A Glimpse of Eternity? Near Death Experiences and the Hope of Future Life, *The Modern Churchman* 30/3 (1988) 25.

[26] *ST* 3a 2, 6 ad 2

[27] Locke, *An Essay Concerning Human Understanding* II c. 27, 14.

[28] *De Ente et Essentia* c.5 (Leonine ed. XLIII, 378).

[29] *Quaestiones de Anima* q.1 as 2.

[30] *ST* 1a 76, I ad 6.

[31] *Contra Gentiles* IV c.81, paragraph 5.

[32] *ST* 3a 54, 3 ad 1.

[33] *1 Cor.* 15, 46.

[34] *Acts* 24, 15.

[35] *Commentarium Super I ad Corinthos* c. XV lect. 2.

CONCLUSION

In the foregoing chapters, we have seen how by asking about the origin of life and the mind we may, by reason, come to the view that human nature includes the soul, and that this soul is not to be explained by evolution. In the first place, as scientists are unable to demonstrate that life has risen from matter by itself, we cannot show that life can be explained by evolution. When writers invoke design in their own theories of evolution, they all too easily overlook the need for a designer. Even if consciousness can be explained by the evolution of the nervous system, this still is not enough to explain the human mind. The mind is not just a further development of consciousness by evolution, because our ability to speak, reason, understand and reflect on ourselves constitutes an unbridgeable gap between us and the rest of animals. Using language with rules and thinking logically, that is according to valid rules of reasoning, cannot be explained by evolution, which proceeds by chance mutations, because doing things with rules is contrary to the very idea of chance. As language is not explained by evolution, nor is thought, which words presuppose. Self-reflection cannot be explained materially or scientifically, because nothing material can reflect *on* itself.

As these abilities set us quite apart from all other animals, we are not merely continuous with nature, as any purely evolutionary view of human beings requires us to be; nor are we simply products of evolution. We do well to recall the conclusion of Alfred Wallace, that our intellectual nature has another immediate source than our physiological nature. As Aristotle discerned, the mind 'comes in from outside', because it is not a power of matter.[1] We should not merely speak of 'the ascent of man', as though we have wholly risen from below by evolution, but also of a 'descent of man' from above, whence comes the soul with the power of understanding. As we have not merely risen from below but have intellectual powers which do not result from our physiology alone, we have an existence that *transcends* the power of matter. We would not transcend our physical nature, as we do, if we were merely generated by it.

Because we transcend the body, our existence can continue beyond it. The soul is immortal, because we see that the mind, which is a power of it, has a certain independence of the body in two ways. First, although things are going on in the brain when we think, thoughts cannot be correlated one to one with physical events in the brain. And secondly, although we require the brain for receiving the data of our thinking, thinking on the data in a general and universal way is not itself a power of the brain. Since we transcend the body in the way we can think of things generally, whereas the senses only know things individually, the human soul transcends the body and need not perish with it.

As it has a power and activity above that of the body, it is something subsistent, which could exist by its own activity. The alternative view of the mind is that it is a complex of mental states or is identical with its contents, but if the mind is just its contents, this does not explain how it is something that *acts* and can reflect on itself. The mind and soul also seem to be above the body, because we can reflect *on* our actions.

One person to draw attention to the transcendence of human beings in recent times has been Keith Ward. Ward, however, tries to combine this with an evolutionary account of human beings. But it is quite inconsistent to hold that human life is part of a continuous process which has emerged from simpler forms of life *and* that our life is transcendent, for how can we transcend the body if we have merely risen from below? Ward thinks that *quantum* theory will explain how mental states have emerged from the physical structure of the brain. This view is similar to the one put forward by Roger Penrose in *Shadows of the Mind*. But Gerald Edelman, a neurophysiologist

and Nobel Prize winner, thinks that this is a blind alley.[2] Ward
says that 'the soul is the subject of these (mental) states', but why
should he think that they need a special subject if thought arises
from the brain by physical activity?[3] And where does this soul
come from if it does not come from the body? Although Ward
says that the soul is brought into being by natural processes, he
also thinks that its most important characteristic is its capacity
for transcendence.[4] By this he means the capacity to exist, to
stand outside the physical processes that generate it. But the
soul that comes from matter rises no higher than the powers of
the matter from which it is drawn. We cannot transcend nature
if we are merely generated by it. Since Ward thinks that this
capacity for transcendence is quite new and distinct, he can
hardly think it has come about by evolution, in which there are
no great jumps.

Ward also believes that the soul finds its fulfilment beyond
this world. As he recognizes that our conscious states cannot
exist separately without a subject when we have died, he needs
the soul for the next life. Obviously, the subject of conscious
states in the next life needs to be the same as in this life, if the
same person is to remain. But the soul that has been generated
by the body cannot continue apart from it. The logic of Ward's
position was spelled out long ago by St Thomas Aquinas: if the
soul is not created, it is dependent on matter; if it is dependent
on matter, it cannot be immortal.[5] We do not have a truly
transcendent existence unless the soul survives the body.

The human soul is immortal, because it is immaterial;
unless it were immaterial, the mind could not reflect on itself.
We have deprived ourselves, however, of the means of showing
that the mind is immaterial, because it is now common to call
any form of conscious life, including sensation, 'mental'. Thus
there no longer seems to be any great difference between the
mind and sensation, with the result that it is widely thought
they can both be explained in the same way, materially. We
need once again to recover the original meaning of the word
'mental', which is properly for what is in the mind. The mind
that thinks with concepts is more than the imagination; so it is
not to be explained merely by the way we get images. Moreover,

we have lost the right to call anything 'psychological', unless we truly have a soul (*psuche*).

Although some prefer to replace the soul with the self, this creates as many problems as it is meant to solve, for it implies a dualist view of human beings. If what I am is a self plus a body, then a self, which is a person, is a part of what I am, whereas surely a person is what I am as a whole. As I am a human being and I am a person, a person is a human being, who is someone with a body. The person is not a part but the whole.

Since the body is an essential part of what I am, the human person does not return to a permanent existence after this life unless the body is raised up again one day. However, neither is the *same* person raised up unless the soul is immortal, for there is no identity without some continuity of existence, which is of the soul after the body has died. Thus the resurrection requires the immortality of the soul. When writers with Christian faith leave out the soul, the price they pay for avoiding dualism is too high, since it precludes the immortality of the soul that belief in the resurrection requires. When these writers omit the soul, they do not sufficiently consider what explains the mind if it is not a power of the body. We need the soul, however, even for this life, to explain the mind, which is not a power of matter. We should also be reluctant to discard the soul, since it is, after all, what makes us in the image of God. We have no need, however, to omit the soul in order to escape dualism, since there is a way of retaining the unity of the human being, even though the soul be subsistent, because the body and soul have a *substantial union*. The body is not even a human substance without the soul, which gives it its life and unity. A human being has a unity, because that by which we think is also that by which we have life and move, for the mind is a power of the soul.

Our destiny corresponds with our origin. Since that which makes us intelligent beings does not rise from matter but comes from above, our end lies beyond this world. The reason why we return to God as our everlasting end is that we come from him.

NOTES

[1]   *De Generatione et Corruptione* II c.3, 736 b 28.
[2]   *Bright Air, Brilliant Fire* (Penguin 1992) 217.
[3]   *Defending the Soul* (Oxford 1992) 145.
[4]   *Ibid.* 142.
[5]   *ST* 1a 118, 2 central reply.

INDEX